MASSIVE

THE STORY OF WEST HAM'S
EUROPA CONFERENCE LEAGUE WINNING SEASON

MASSIVE

THE MIRACLE OF PRAGUE

PETE MAY

First published in Great Britain in 2024 by
Biteback Publishing Ltd, London

ISBN 978-1-78590-852-1

10 9 8 7 6 5 4 3 2 1

A CIP catalogue record for this book is available from the British Library.

Set in Minion Pro and Alternate Gothic Condensed

Printed and bound in Great Britain by
CPI Group (UK) Ltd, Croydon CR0 4YY

ALSO BY PETE MAY

Summit for the Weekend

What Are Words Worth?

Man About Tarn

Goodbye to Boleyn

Whovian Dad

The Joy of Essex

World Cup Expert: Teams

World Cup Expert: Players

Flying So High: West Ham's Cup Finals

There's a Hippo in My Cistern

Hammers in the Heart

Ageing Body, Confused Mind

Football and its Followers

Rent Boy

West Ham: Irons in the Soul

Sunday Muddy Sunday

The Lad Done Bad (with Denis Campbell and Andrew Shields)

CONTENTS

WE'RE ON THE MARCH WITH LYALL'S ARMY

MAY 1980

West Ham are at Wembley again. I'm a twenty-year-old post-punk doing an English degree at the University of Lancaster. Being 300-odd miles from Upton Park, I've not been able to join the queues at the ground for FA Cup final tickets. But with the optimism of youth, I withdraw the final £40 left of my student grant and decide to travel back to Essex and go to Wembley, hoping to buy a ticket from a tout. My final exams start in three days' time, but even so, I have to be there. Plenty of revision has been done, 40 per cent of my degree is coursework and if I don't know my subjects by now, I never will. So, on Friday night it's a train from Lancaster back to my parents' house.

On the day of the final, I travel up to Wembley by tube

with the two Steves from Brentwood, who do have tickets. Wembley Way is full of klaxons going off, crates of beer and fans in white, claret and blue scarves. Outside the turnstile I start asking if anyone has a spare ticket. Miraculously, a fan with a small boy suggests that if he can sneak his son under the turnstile, I can have his ticket for a fiver. This is a bargain, as the face value is only £3.50. This piece of East End gamesmanship works splendidly, and I'm soon through the turnstile and inside the stadium, thanking my saviour profusely. Everyone is singing and drinking bottles of beer in the concourse. Then it's up the steps towards the sunlight and the luminous green grass before taking my place on the terraces.

I'm wearing my black Harrington jacket, blue Levi's jeans, a replica West Ham Admiral shirt and a white scarf with claret and blue trimming. My programme costs 80p and features adverts for Skol, Player's No. 6, Littlewoods Pools and Kevin Keegan's new column in the *Sunday Mirror*. Wembley is moving into merchandising, and a programme advert offers Wembley-branded keyrings, wristbands, sweaters, executive jotters and programme binders. The hoardings around the pitch advertise Rizla, Talbot, Hotpoint, Mornflake Oats, DAF Trucks, National Girobank, Pye Radio, Bush Colour TV, Hitachi, Philips and Sharp. The only cameras are with the men in orange 'press' bibs crouched behind the goals. If you want to use a phone, you will have to leave the stadium and walk around the streets of Wembley looking for a red phone box.

Any West Ham fans reading the *Daily Express* that morning will have been incensed by the comments of Brian Clough. The iconoclastic Nottingham Forest manager has written:

> Trevor Brooking floats like a butterfly… and stings like one. I have never had a high opinion of him as a player. He has been lucky enough to become a member of teams he shouldn't really have had a sniff at. I believe his lack of application and other players like him has meant relegation for West Ham in the past and the failure to win promotion this time.

That's just about completed John Lyall's team talk for him.

These are heady times. The Cockney Rejects are soon to release a wonderfully belligerent version of 'I'm Forever Blowing Bubbles'. The number one single is 'Geno' by Dexys Midnight Runners. The dad of my school friends Alison and Roz has bought something called a video recorder and is going to record the match. Tom Baker is still the Doctor in *Doctor Who*. Nelson Mandela is in a South African prison. Margaret Thatcher is the British Prime Minister but will surely only last one term. Jim Callaghan is still the leader of the Labour Party but looks set to be replaced by either Michael Foot or Denis Healey. The album charts contain works by Boney M, Rose Royce, Suzi Quatro, Genesis, Status Quo, The Undertones and Black Sabbath.

'Trevor Brooking Sells More Dummies than Mothercare,' reads one of the many banners around me. Ugly wire fences at the front of the terrace ensure there won't be any pitch invasions as there were at the 1975 cup final. Other home-made banners read 'Hitchcock's Dead but Psycho Plays On', 'Get your camera off our banner', and the lyrical ballad 'The Greatest Players in the Land are Captain Billy and his Band. That's Frank the Lamp, Alan Dev, Paul and Stewart and Tricky Trev.' Alan Devonshire of West Ham and Pat Rice of Arsenal have also been the source of much punning. The banners include 'Devonshire is the cream, Rice is the pudding', 'Billy Bonds eats Rice' and 'Devonshire is a Delight'.

The West Ham players inspect the pitch wearing brown suits, accompanied by huge cheers. It's a big day for Paul Allen who is set to become the youngest player ever to appear in an FA Cup final at the age of seventeen years and 256 days. The BBC's Bob Wilson interviews the players before the match, though as he talks to Arsenal's Liam Brady a chorus of 'Who the f**king hell are you?' breaks out from the West Ham fans.

There's a brass band, the Combined Bands of the Guards Division, as pre-match entertainment. Then 'Abide with Me' is played, which is always an emotional moment. John Lyall leads his men out in a brown lounge jacket and black trousers. The West Ham players are clad in claret and blue tracksuit tops over their kit. The Duchess of Kent is wearing a purple twinset and hat as she goes to shake hands with the teams. The West Ham and Arsenal fans sing 'Bubbles' and 'There's only one Liam Brady!' respectively.

The game kicks off with West Ham in their white Admiral away kit and Arsenal in yellow. 'We all follow the West Ham over land and sea! We all follow the West Ham on to victory!' echoes around Wembley.

Terry Neill's Arsenal seem puzzled by West Ham's change of formation. John Lyall, who is chain-smoking on the bench, has pulled off a clever tactical coup, playing Stuart Pearson wide on the left and leaving David Cross as a lone striker. Cross works tremendously hard to occupy O'Leary and Young and this confuses the Arsenal defence, while an extra man in midfield helps negate the influence of Arsenal's playmaker, Liam Brady.

Early on, a good run and cross from Stuart Pearson allows Geoff Pike to get in a shot that is saved by Pat Jennings. The crucial moment arrives after thirteen minutes. Alan Devonshire takes on Pat Rice and beats the Arsenal man for speed, sending over a cross that Jennings can only parry. David Cross shoots against a defender, then Pearson miscues, hitting the ball across goal. And there is Trevor Brooking stooping to divert a header past Jennings. The West Ham end erupts, though we're not quite sure who scored since it was at the other end of the stadium.

'We're on the march with Lyall's army! We're all going to Wem-ber-ley! And we'll really shake 'em up when we win the

FA Cup! 'Cos West Ham is the greatest football team!' sing the Hammers fans. The Arsenal fans respond with, 'You only sing when you're winning!'

Bizarrely, West Ham had finished seventh in the Second Division but are giving a jaded Arsenal quite a game. Can this be the same West Ham side that recently lost at home to Shrewsbury? Alvin Martin and Billy Bonds are massive at the back for West Ham. Pike works as hard as ever, the young Allen is doing well in midfield and Frank Lampard is showing all his experience at left-back, having been preferred over the matchday substitute Paul Brush.

In the second half, Arsenal do create a couple of good chances, but Phil Parkes, the Hammers keeper who seems all hair and moustache, saves smartly from Graham Rix and Brian Talbot. The West Ham fans amuse themselves with a not-very-friendly chorus of 'He's only a poor little Gunner / His face is all tattered and torn / He made me feel sick / So I hit him with a brick / And now he don't sing anymore!'

Brooking does a lot of hard tackling and tracking back. In the final minute, he manages to release seventeen-year-old Allen. Allen's through on goal but is crudely hacked down by Young with a cynical professional foul. The referee is only allowed to give a yellow card, as the FA has yet to update its rules on such offences, even though it's a goalscoring opportunity. On the BBC commentary John Motson says, 'Oh what a pity! A cynical foul and fully deserving of the yellow card it got.' Ray Stewart hits the Arsenal wall with the free kick and Young gets away with his professional foul.

The West Ham fans are starting to think it could happen and have started singing 'Bubbles', 'You'll Never Walk Alone' and 'We Shall Not Be Moved'. Brady makes a great run from deep but is tackled on the edge of the area by Brooking, who is making Clough look pretty stupid with his tracking back.

The West Ham fans are whistling for full time. There's another chorus of 'Bubbles'. Rix puts one last ball into the Hammers' box and finally the whistle blows. Cross collapses onto the turf, head in hands. Lyall embraces Bonds, Brooking and Lampard. People are hugging me on the terraces.

Soon, Billy Bonds is leading his men up to the royal box. As he receives his medal, young Allen is in tears, overcome by what he has just achieved. His chairman Len Cearns looks concerned. Bonzo shakes hands with the Duchess of Kent and lifts the FA Cup above his head to a thunderous roar.

Pike has a Hammers scarf around his neck as the players lap the pitch with the cup. 'Lyall, Lyall' chant the Irons fans to the tune of 'Amazing Grace'. Allen is wearing a claret and white cap and holding the cup aloft with Pike, while Stewart holds the lid. Squad players Bobby Ferguson, Jimmy Neighbour and Pat Holland are on the pitch celebrating too. In the team photo, Devonshire is holding a West Ham teddy bear and now the lid of the cup is on Parkes's head. Lyall leaves the celebrations and stands in front of the tunnel. He stays there for a minute, reflecting on the joy of the fans, before heading for the dressing room.

'One team in London! There's only one team in London!' chant the Hammers fans.

Eventually, after all the celebratory mayhem, I meet the two Steves outside. We head to Trafalgar Square for a knees-up by the fountains and stop at a new burger restaurant called McDonald's on Haymarket. We figure the action is more likely to be at Upton Park.

We move on to the Boleyn Tavern near West Ham's ground. All the cars on Green Street are sounding their horns. Inside the packed Boleyn, everyone is singing 'Bubbles'. An Arsenal scarf is lit with a cigarette lighter and burned in the centre of the front bar, which would probably not win the approval of the fire brigade. Beer is drunk and the carpet gets stickier. We head off to take the tube to Liverpool Street and the last train back to Brentwood.

After a long night, I stumble towards my parents' house in Great Warley, exiting Brentwood station with the chorus of 'We're on the march with Lyall's army!' still going through my head. I don't seem to notice the two-mile walk home.

The next day, I travel back to Lancaster for my final exams. The fellow student who gives me a lift is an Arsenal fan, which makes it even better. West Ham will surely win promotion next season. At the age of twenty, I've seen us win the FA Cup twice in five years, plus we reached the European

Cup Winners' Cup final in 1976. Never mind mighty Liverpool. With Brooking, Bonds, Parkes and Devonshire, anything is possible. West Ham will surely become a major force in the game. Next season we'll be competing in Europe. And it won't be long until the next trophy.

1

SLOW STARTERS

AUGUST 2022

Up against Manchester City... what could possibly go wrong? It's a sweltering August afternoon as West Ham's Premier League season begins unusually early on 7 August, in order to accommodate the December World Cup in Qatar.

Manager David Moyes has made real progress at West Ham. In his first spell at the club, he arrived halfway through the 2017–18 season and saved the side from relegation by installing a system of solid defending and converting winger Marko Arnautović into a highly effective striker. But that wasn't enough for the board, who failed to renew his short-term contract and installed the more glamorous figure of Manuel Pellegrini, a Chilean coach who had won the Premier League with Manchester City.

Pellegrini finished tenth in his first season at West Ham.

But by Christmas 2019, the Irons were struggling in the relegation zone. Mark Noble and young Declan Rice were often outnumbered in midfield, and Pellegrini had bought several expensive attacking players on big wages who were underperforming, such as Felipe Anderson, Andriy Yarmolenko, Sébastien Haller, Albian Ajeti and the injury-prone Jack Wilshere.

The West Ham board were big enough to admit they had made a mistake in letting Moyes go and invited him back to save the Hammers again. The Scot, who seems to have a penchant for converting wingers into strikers, turned Michail Antonio into a one-man forward line, using his strength and speed to build a side around. He made a couple of astute signings in Jarrod Bowen and Tomáš Souček, in a bid to instil some pace and durability in the side. Covid meant the latter part of the season was played behind closed doors, but after a late Yarmolenko winner against Chelsea, the team survived.

Moyes surprised everyone by taking the side to sixth place in 2020–21 and getting West Ham into the Europa League. He made solid signings in Vladimír Coufal and Craig Dawson, got a gifted maverick in Saïd Benrahma and pulled off a great loan deal for Jesse Lingard from Manchester United. West Ham played a low block but counter-attacked at speed. The style wasn't to everyone's taste, but at times it was thrilling to see convincing away wins, particularly when Lingard ran from his own half to score against Wolves. Rice was the best young player in England and had replaced Noble as captain. For a time, the Hammers even looked likely to make the top four, though an over-reliance on the fitness of Antonio and a small squad told in the end. But it was a great season and a sign of real progress.

After lockdown, the fans returned to the London Stadium in 2021–22. The ends of the ground had been squared off and it was starting to feel more like home. On an emotional night beneath the lights, West Ham beat Leicester City 4–1 with Antonio starring and scoring twice. Kurt Zouma was signed from Chelsea to strengthen the defence. West Ham were back in Europe and topped their Europa League group. The Irons achieved statement wins at home to Liverpool and Chelsea and moved into the top four at the halfway stage.

A great run in the Europa League followed. West Ham overturned a 1–0 away leg deficit to defeat six-time winners Sevilla 2–0, on the best night in the London Stadium's short history. The noise was magnificent, and the fact West Ham's winner came from Ukrainian Yarmolenko, so soon after his country was invaded by Russia, only added to the emotion.

After a home draw with Lyon, the side astonishingly won 3–0 in France thanks to goals from Dawson, Rice and Bowen and advanced to the semi-final. Could this be the season when West Ham finally win a trophy, we wondered? In the semi-final against Eintracht Frankfurt, the German side scored in the first minute at the London Stadium to rapidly puncture West Ham's bubbles. It ended 2–1 to Frankfurt, though it might have been different if Bowen's effort hadn't hit the underside of the bar in added time. West Ham still had some hope in the second leg, but after Aaron Cresswell was sent off for denying a goalscoring opportunity after nineteen minutes, Frankfurt edged to a nervy 1–0 win against West Ham's ten men.

It was a glorious failure in Europe and a sense that our best chance of a trophy in years had gone. The side's form had trailed off in the league since Christmas, with the small squad overstretched by the European run. The big signing of Nikola Vlašić had been disappointing. West Ham could have finished sixth and made the Europa League again, but on the final day of the season, they allowed Brighton to come back from Antonio's goal and win 3–1, leaving the Hammers in seventh place and in the Europa Conference League. Moyes was visibly angry and suggested that changes would be made – though some fans felt that he had perhaps got all he could out of a tired squad and that these players couldn't keep overachieving forever.

And so, come August 2022, it has been a summer of rebuilding at the London Stadium. Moyes has signed Italian striker Gianluca Scamacca for around £30 million, which is big money for the Hammers. Will he finally solve the Irons's longstanding striker problem? The West Ham website posts a video entitled 'West Ham Gazzetta', a homage to Channel

4's Italian football coverage featuring James Richardson interviewing Scamacca.

The big man's English is excellent from his time in the Netherlands with PSV Eindhoven, so that should help him settle in at Rush Green. We learn that he has already mastered 'Wotcha, me old China' and 'Come on you Irons!' so that sounds promising. Luca speaks with some articulacy and seems to relish the 'project' at the London Stadium. Hopefully, it will all be Di Canio-esque rather than Zaza-esque as West Ham's record of signing strikers has been abysmal in recent seasons.

The other big signing is £30 million Moroccan defender Nayef Aguerd. Except, this being West Ham, Aguerd has immediately been crocked in a pre-season friendly against Rangers and might be out for three months. Winger Maxwel Cornet, who scored nine goals for Burnley last season, has also arrived for £17.5 million, and looking at some of his cracking volleys from last season, he seems an exciting signing.

In midfield, Flynn Downes has been signed for £12 million from Championship side Swansea City and is championed by the club website as 'one of our own' even though he comes from the East End of, erm, Brentwood in Essex, which is the hometown of both myself and my fellow season ticket-holder Nigel. The other arrival is £10 million goalkeeper Alphonse Areola, the likely successor to Łukasz Fabiański between the sticks. These additions are welcome, though more players are still needed.

On the negative side, skipper Rice only has two years of his contract left to run and it doesn't look like he's going to sign another deal. So, it seems likely that he will be sold in the summer. He's one of the best players in his position in Europe and wants to play in the Champions League. We'll need to have a phenomenal season to keep him.

So, another season begins with my faithful group of West Ham fans. We are perhaps an ageing squad, having been together since the days of the East Stand at Upton Park.

Nigel is newly retired from his day job on *The i* and is devoting himself to heavy metal and prog rock concerts, groundhopping, researching football trivia, watching *Carry On* films, visiting Felixstowe FC and memorising obscure by-election results. Like myself, he has also been known to bag Wainwright fells in the Lake District. For millennia, Nigel has carried a banana to eat at half-time, which my blog has somewhat erroneously claimed to be lucky. He is probably the sole Hammer in leafy Kew Gardens.

Michael is our Renaissance man. He wrote the biography of Nicholas Courtney, who played the Brigadier in *Doctor Who*, and is also an authority on Ted Heath's relationship with Margaret Thatcher, having written a play on the subject. He's written a musical about Soft Cell, plus several other plays, and has been known to use Shakespearean insults at games, such as 'Damn your eyes, ref!' Plus, he's got a Jonathan Spector West Ham shirt as well as a seat from the Boleyn Ground.

Fraser is the most venerable of our number. He once earned a chant of 'There's only one Adam Faith!' due to his resemblance to the singer and actor while at a UEFA Cup game in Palermo. A man who once went to a party with Jack Nicholson, he recently completed a creative writing MA and is now devoting his time to becoming the Raymond Chandler of East London. He is, how shall we put it, a Moyes sceptic. Still longing for the silky football of Ron Greenwood and John Lyall, Fraser would be happy with Pep Guardiola in charge, or even Marcelo Bielsa, but not someone like Moyes who favours counter-attacking football and only plays one striker.

Matt is someone who will attend any game going and speaks movingly of the Dripping Pan at Lewes, among other obscure stadia. He has seen matches from the Faroe Islands to Uzbekistan and regards a romantic minibreak as a trip to Bolton or Wigan with his partner Lisa. He often dispenses copies of *When Saturday Comes* at games. Matt's mum is a vicar, though he uses decidedly ungodly language when frustrated by the likes of Arthur Masuaku or Vlašić. He rivals Nigel on the football trivia and groundhopping front and seems to be permanently at gigs, the theatre or art shows when not at football.

The newest recruit to our season ticket squad is Lisa, who

is a subeditor by day, as well as an avid competition enterer and the number-one fan of Bucks Fizz. We fear that Lisa might have Stockholm Syndrome after living with Matt for so long, as she's started to go to more games than he does. She is an authority on the West Ham Under-21s, the Under-18s and the women's team, as well as being a calming influence on Matt when Benrahma dribbles instead of shoots.

My home team consists of my wife Nicola, who strangely prefers paddleboarding and horse riding to football but puts up with my mood swings after games and seems to understand my strange addiction. My youngest daughter Nell is back at home, having graduated from university. As a child, she once asked why all the West Ham fans were calling Marlon Harewood an 'anchor' after he missed a penalty against Watford. My eldest daughter Lola is currently living in Edinburgh. I took her to her first game at the age of four and she asked whether if someone got a ladder and put the ball on the roof of the stand it would be a straight red card. It probably would I said, though that was before the advent of VAR, which would probably overturn it. They were both at the Championship play-off final at Wembley when West Ham beat Blackpool in 2012 but have not seen West Ham win a major trophy in their lifetimes.

So now the team that meets in caffs is back. Once it was Ken's Cafe in Green Street. The closest approximation we have found in Stratford is the Best Meze cafe on the Broadway. In the cafe, Michael and Nigel are ordering double halloumi baguettes and chips for a tardy Matt and Lisa.

We're discussing how Matt worked his customary magic on the Lionesses at the European Championship final by saying that England haven't done much at corners just before Chloe Kelly scored. Meanwhile, Lisa is making her debut as a season ticket holder today.

Nigel is full of interesting stats from *The Times*, including the fact that Vlašić tops the list for appearances without playing a full ninety minutes last season and that Brighton are playing four teams called United in their first four fixtures (Manchester, Newcastle, West Ham and Leeds) for the first time in forty-eight years. Not a lot of people know that.

We now have a set route to the stadium. Over Stratford Broadway, through Matt's shortcut by the block of flats and down the alley into Carpenters Road (though Nigel prefers the route past the newspaper recycling and the Greenwich Meridian marker on Stratford High Street). On Carpenters Road, fans drink cans of beer by the corner shop and Belly Busters burger stall has now set out its wares. We can see the ArcelorMittal Orbit, a sort of twisted Eiffel Tower made to mark the 2012 London Olympics. Then under the railway bridge where everyone shouts 'Irons!' Along the wide pathway to the stadium, right past the Podium Bar and then a dash to the security gates where we're searched for suspect devices, offensive weapons or, in Nigel's case, a dodgy lucky banana.

There's almost a disaster as we arrive at the stadium only to see the last programme being sold. Matt remains Zen-like, but Nigel and I desperately search inside the security zone for more and eventually find a last box on sale in the West Ham tent. Nigel barges into the queue, elbows aside a few children and grannies and manages to buy our programmes – even though the price has gone up from £3.50 to four quid. What will our new Prime Minister do to tackle programme inflation?

We pass through the electronic turnstiles at block H. Inside the stadium, we're joined by Fraser wearing a natty Albert Steptoe/David Essex-style neckerchief, possibly in celebration of Moyes finally buying a striker. Sadder news is that Clacton-based Alison and Scott from the row behind us have retired along with Mark Noble, though West Ham will surely buy them back for a massive fee in a few years' time.

At the City match there's a centre-back injury crisis, with Aguerd, Angelo Ogbonna and Dawson all out, Issa Diop wanting to leave and Ben Johnson played as an emergency stopper alongside Zouma. Scamacca is on the bench, but none of the new signings are in the starting line-up, with Aguerd injured and Areola, Cornet and Downes all substitutes.

West Ham have a decent first two minutes, force a corner and then see Antonio head over from Pablo Fornals's cross. After that, City take control, with full-backs João Cancelo and Kyle Walker pushed into midfield and Manuel Lanzini, Fornals, Souček and Rice outnumbered and out-thought.

City's new striker Erling Haaland is so huge he looks rather like Ted Hughes's *The Iron Giant* but clad in a blond wig. Haaland almost gets his head to Phil Foden's cross as it becomes attack versus defence. The Grealish Sniper (so named because of Jack's penchant for going to ground) reappears as City's winger starts tumbling theatrically to the floor whenever tackled. Fabiański has to go off after injuring his hip while making a brave punch and is replaced by Areola.

When İlkay Gündoğan plays Haaland through, the substitute keeper hesitates for a second and then brings down the £51 million striker. Haaland confidently dispatches the penalty and does a sit-down meditation celebration – possibly in honour of Matt's new-found indifference to pleasure, pain and programme collecting.

At half-time, Nigel eats his 'lucky' banana, and the Irons have a slightly better start to the second half. The key moment comes when Rice gets under the ball and fires over the bar when he probably should have scored.

Subs Scamacca and Benrahma at least give City something different to think about. The big Italian tests Ederson with a fine header, only for it to be ruled offside. He is a handful, and despite his lack of pre-season games, it looks like he can adapt quickly to the Premier League. Benrahma also tests Ederson with a low shot, but with space now available, the inevitable happens. Rodri finds Kevin De Bruyne, who dissects the West Ham centre-backs with a fine ball. Haaland shifts the ball on to his left foot and strokes home. 'We're not really here!' sing the away fans.

After that, it's a question of how many City will get on a very hot afternoon. It's been a strangely passive performance against a great team. When I remark that our pressing game isn't working, Michael says, quite accurately, 'We're playing a de-pressing game.'

There's nearly a fight behind us as the overly aggressive fan who has been giving expletive-laden advice to the side to 'Just f***ing run!' (not that wise in 27-degree weather) is told to just say it in his head by a man whose patience has snapped. There's a lot of Boris-style bluster as Matt, the vicar's son, asks, 'Why can't some fans just stay positive?'

Haaland misses a good chance to get a hat-trick, and Conor Coventry and Downes make their Premier League debuts in a minute-long cameo. West Ham scored in every home league game last season, and now that record has been blown in one match. To be fair, the Irons have been without the much-missed Dawson and Aguerd, while Scamacca and Cornet will surely improve the side. This result does not define our season, and at least we only have to play City once more.

We walk across the wide highways of the Queen Elizabeth Olympic Park, past Stratford International and down the not-very-aptly-named Victory Parade to The Eagle at Leyton. It's taken us a long time to settle on a pub since the ground move. The Tap at Stratford International was too busy. On Stratford Broadway we tried the Refreshment Room, which was all right even if it took a long time to get served, but it wasn't quite a real pub. Ye Olde Black Bull was always rammed, even if it occasionally did Titanic Plum Porter. The Cart and Horses had something for Nigel, being the first pub where Iron Maiden played, but it was pricey and a bit of a trek. We tried the King Edward, which was a bit lairy and the Wetherspoons, which felt too lowbrow. The Railway on Leyton Road was an isolated Victorian building among the *Blade Runner* metropolis but always felt rather rundown. The Neighbourhood Bar was too modern and too like a continental bar for our set of discerning pub connoisseurs. We'd also flirted with the bar at the Stratford Theatre Royal, which suited Michael but wasn't really a football venue, though it did have some good stage props. Oh, and there was a barge on the River Lee Navigation that for a time provided bottled Doom Bar.

Our team even tried some craft beer places in Hackney

Wick but Nigel, ever the traditionalist, drew the line at glasses that only held two thirds of a pint and the myriad hoppy hipster ales at Tank Bar. Matt and Lisa were more amenable to the Lord Napier Star, the rebuilt pub by Hackney Wick Overground station, which has a roof terrace where after the Spurs match we listened to the choruses of 'Tottenham get battered!' It used to be abandoned and famously had the phrase 'from shithouse to penthouse' daubed on its front.

We discovered The Eagle one evening after my shortcut to find The Railway went wrong and we stumbled upon it in the back streets of Leyton. For once, everyone seemed to like it. The Eagle is a decent boozer with plenty of room and friendly staff, plus The Who on the jukebox and football on the TV. It might sell mainly Guinness and lager on tap, but after a little persuasion and a promise to become regulars, their fridge now has an array of bottled beers for craft-beer aficionados.

We split a round and head to the beer garden. Inspired by the fracas behind us at the London Stadium, Matt reminisces about rows between our own supporters, including the time a fan announced that Matty Etherington was the worst player he had ever seen, only to be quickly corrected with a list of numerous West Ham non-legends. After a second beer, I head home to have dinner with my wife Nicola, who has long maintained that she can tell West Ham's results by my gait as I come through the front door.

After the match, a downbeat Moyes is, as always, honest

and says, 'They were so good today. Both their full-backs played like midfield players today and it caused us problems.' The games against Forest and Brighton will give a better idea of how the season will go. But this was nothing like the team that disrupted City in the 2–2 draw at the end of last season, and a rapid improvement is needed.

For the second fixture of the season, the Irons are at newly promoted Nottingham Forest. The Forest line-up includes Jesse Lingard, who has very publicly snubbed Moyes's approaches in favour of more 'love' at Nottingham. The Hammers start well, with Benrahma's drive forcing a save from Dean Henderson, and Souček almost getting to the rebound, only to be denied by a great saving tackle from Harry Toffolo.

Then Benrahma scores, following a fine through ball from Rice, only for the goal to be disallowed after VAR detects Antonio blocking Orel Mangala in the build-up. After that, Forest take a lucky lead, with Lingard probing and Johnson's clearance hitting Taiwo Awoniyi's shin and rebounding into the back of the net.

In the second half, West Ham pepper Forest's goal. Fornals hits a screamer on to the bar, with Souček's header from the rebound then being denied by a save from Henderson. Benrahma smacks a brilliant free kick on to the angle of post and bar, with the ball bouncing on the Forest line and back into Henderson's hands.

An equaliser looks inevitable when the Hammers win a

penalty. Benrahma finds Souček, whose goal-bound shot is handballed away by McKenna. Penalty king Noble has retired, so skipper Rice takes responsibility for the spot-kick, but his slightly scuffed low shot is not hard enough and is saved by Henderson who turns to the home fans, clenching his fists in celebration. Even after that there's another big chance from a corner, with Zouma's header being cleared off the line.

Matt's WhatsApp commentary reads like the modern version of a Samuel Beckett script on the futility of life:

> So Beni hit the bar with a fantastic free kick, the ref missed a blatant handball in the box and failed to send off the culprit and Deccers missed the penalty ... We are literally never going to score this season. You all know I hate to criticise referees but he's having a shocker ... We need a goal so genius Moyes takes off Bowen and Antonio and gives Cornet five minutes ... Crisis club West Ham, no points, no goals only Manchester United managing to be worse than us.

So, it's two defeats in a row for the Hammers, but in a weird way this defeat is encouraging, in particular the return to form from Benrahma. We really should have buried Forest. I'm hopeful that the lads can get some confidence against Viborg on Thursday and then finally beat bogey team Brighton in the must-win game on Sunday.

The penalty-taking situation needs to be resolved. Rice has missed two out of his three penalties for West Ham and really should be relieved of the job. He's a great player but not always a great striker of the ball – a lot of his shots go over the bar as we saw with the chance he missed against Man City, though he does get some long-range screamers too. Sometimes he takes too much on as captain and he doesn't need the pressure of taking penalties too. Benrahma or Antonio might be better options.

Meanwhile, the rebuild continues with defender Thilo Kehrer signing from Paris Saint-Germain (PSG) for £10.1 million, which seems relatively cheap. He sounds like an upgrade on Diop, who has been sold to Fulham. The German international has won three Ligue 1 titles, three cups and played in a Champions League final with PSG. At twenty-five he is a good age, and with just one year left on his contract he comes at a bargain price for a centre-back – compare his price with the £80 million Manchester United paid for Harry Maguire. Another advantage is his versatility. Kehrer is mainly a centre-back but can also play both full-back positions and defensive midfield, which in a small squad is going to prove very useful. Looking at his interview on the club website, he seems a level-headed individual and should be a good addition.

Thursday night sees the club's first game in the Europa Conference League play-offs against Viborg of Denmark.

This is not a team many of us have heard of, and thinking back to *Star Trek: The Next Generation*, there's a slight worry we might all be assimilated by the Viborg.

Will Europe's third-best competition prove a distraction? Moyes has vowed to take the competition seriously but the number of games is going to be gruelling if we are to win it. Though when did West Ham last win anything? The disappointment of last season's Europa League semi-final defeat still hurts.

'[The tournament] is an absolutely fantastic thing. We finished seventh in the league last year and the fact people are talking about Europe is good,' says a positive Moyes. 'There are so many teams in the league who would shake your hand and thank you for European football. It is a great thing for West Ham. We have a play-off, and we want to get through.'

In contrast, Tottenham never seemed to place much emphasis on the Europa Conference League when they participated in 2021–22. They were eliminated after they were unable to field a team in Rennes following a Covid outbreak. They also managed to lose games to Paços de Ferreira, Vitesse Arnhem and NŠ Mura.

The inaugural competition of 2021–22 was won by José Mourinho's Roma. It was significant that the former 'special one' clearly valued the tournament. Mourinho was in tears at the final whistle and clutched the trophy like it was his dearest possession. For clubs just outside the elite, the trophy was a chance to make memories. Roma had ended a 61-year wait for a European title.

Mourinho compared it to his other great triumphs:

> Winning with Manchester United, even if it wasn't the strongest version of United, is something normal. Winning the Champions League with Porto is not normal. Winning the Champions League with Inter brought satisfaction to their fans, and today with Roma we made history … I am a Porto fan, an Inter fan, a Chelsea fan. I am crazy about Real Madrid; I am now a Roma fan. I belong to all those clubs because we had these moments together.

Although 30,230 tickets have been sold for the Viborg game at the London Stadium, the crowd is a lot less than the official figure. Thanks to a train strike, most fans from Essex haven't turned up – the Central line is also dodgy, and a tube strike is due for Friday. Diehards Matt and Lisa have been in the Best Cafe beforehand, and Fraser is also there early. Michael is away spending more time with his musicals, perhaps fearing that West Ham are playing a team of cyborgs from *The Terminator*. There's a good contingent of away fans living Danishly, bouncing up and down, going shirtless and chanting throughout what is apparently the biggest game in their history.

It's an experimental Hammers side, with Scamacca and

Cornet starting and Coventry and Harrison Ashby getting games, plus a welcome return for Angelo Ogbonna. Viborg are fielding Jay-Roy Grot, perhaps as a tribute to all the grot we've seen at the London Stadium over the years. And in one of the few positive things to come out of Brexit, Viborg have been unable to get visas for two of their African players thanks to government red tape.

Early on, Scamacca tests the keeper, and after being released by Ashby, Bowen cuts inside to chip over the keeper and just wide. A tardy Nigel arrives, having walked from Cambridge Heath carrying a huge sausage, perhaps in place of his lucky banana. The Irons take the lead as Cornet twists his full-back one way, then another, and sends over a perfect cross for Scamacca to rise above his defender and power home a header. Hopefully it's the first of many for the Italian.

Scamacca has another long-range effort saved, and Viborg have chances too, shooting just wide and causing Areola to race smartly from his goal to foil a one-on-one with Grot. At the other end, Ashby forces Lucas Lund to tip over a fierce shot.

The game seems safe after sixty-four minutes as Bowen latches on to a loose ball and scores with a quick low shot from distance, fooling Lund who was probably expecting a pass. Kehrer, Benrahma and Antonio come on, but the triple substitution unsettles West Ham a little, as almost immediately Viborg get in a cross from the left. The Hammers's defence has not been expecting Mr Bonde, who scores with an unopposed header.

Areola has to make an excellent tip over to prevent a Viborg equaliser. Thankfully, Benrahma carries on his good form from the Forest match, making a great run down the left, getting to the byline and pulling back for Antonio to tap home. We've seen three key players get off the mark in Scamacca, Bowen and Antonio, which should be good for the Brighton game.

After the final whistle, we make an unusually quick exit to Ye Olde Black Bull. There's no Titanic Plum Porter, though a pint of Tribute goes down well. Then it's a dash with Nigel to the Central line and a quick discussion about Wainwright bagging before he departs for a long day's journey into night back to Kew.

It's always good to secure the first win of the season, and Scamacca has now scored more than Simone Zaza, our last big-name Italian striker. There's still work to do in the second leg, but a two-goal lead should be enough.

But then, along come Brighton. We're up against a team that we haven't beaten in ten Premier League games. From Hackney Wick station I head to a sunny London Stadium, walking past fans drinking outside Tank and on to White Post Lane. Here a sign advertises Skeeter's Axe Throwing, a sport that might well have appealed to the West Ham Inter City Firm in their heyday. Then it's alongside the River Lee

Navigation, full of barges offering drinks and food, over the bridge and through the security checks.

I sit by the giant Olympic Bell to read my programme. The bronze Olympic Bell was designed by the Whitechapel Bell Foundry, cast in the Netherlands and installed in 2012. It's the largest bell in the world, apparently. Bradley Wiggins opened the 2012 Olympics by pressing a button to ring it. On the bell is inscribed part of Caliban's speech from *The Tempest*: 'Be not afeard; the isle is full of noises.' This seems a rather apt description for what happens when West Ham lose at home.

Inside the stadium, we learn that Matt and Lisa have been to the Royal Academy summer show in search of great art (not often seen at the London Stadium); Michael has returned to the fold; Nigel is carrying his 'lucky' AFC Wimbledon bag; and Fraser's season ticket didn't work at the turnstile. Sadly for him, a steward then let him in.

Nigel's copy of *The Times* is full of bad omens, pointing out that 'ten winless matches against Brighton is the most West Ham have registered against a single opponent without victory' and that should the Hammers lose their first three matches without scoring, it will be the side's worst start since 1971–72. 'What could possibly go right?' quips Michael.

West Ham play reasonably well for ten minutes, with Benrahma cutting inside and sending a drive just wide. Fornals finds Bowen on the wing with a fine ball, but his cross is just behind Antonio. Then Brighton start to keep the ball and exert a familiar voodoo over the Hammers. It all goes wrong after twenty-two minutes as Zouma steps out of defence, runs upfield, takes a heavy touch and loses possession. Leandro Trossard sends Danny Welbeck away, and caught out by the speed of the break, debutant Kehrer brings down the former Man United man. Alexis Mac Allister dispatches the penalty.

West Ham are playing with a curious lack of energy, with Rice and Souček unable to impose themselves in midfield, Antonio toiling and Bowen not able to get on the ball. Łukasz Fabiański gives the ball to Zouma every time, but he's our least comfortable player on the ball. Graham Potter's Brighton look a very well-coached team, despite the summer sales of Yves Bissouma and Marc Cucurella.

'This is the difference between a season when Bowen is on fire and a season when he isn't,' counsels Nigel. Matt remarks that Brighton are a pound shop Man City in the way they keep possession. We decide that if City are the equivalent of Waitrose, then Brighton are Tesco (hence the Tesco bag kit), and West Ham are probably Aldi.

The Irons start the second half with more intensity, as Cresswell has a goal-bound shot blocked and Fornals tests Robert Sánchez after a good move. But again, West Ham concede at just the wrong time. Pascal Groß flicks the ball round a bamboozled Zouma while Trossard wasn't being tracked, and the Brighton man finishes calmly to seal the result.

Scamacca and Cornet come on, but the pattern of the game remains the same as fellow sub Lanzini seems to misplace all his passes and Brighton send a free header over the bar. For six minutes, Scamacca and Antonio are up front as a pairing, though Moyes soon takes Antonio off. The out-of-form Souček sticks at it at least, forcing a tip over from Sánchez with a late header. From the resulting corner, the Brighton keeper then makes another excellent save from Souček's header.

If Brighton played us every week, they'd be top of the league. The match has been rather like the *Doctor Who* story 'Heaven Sent', where Peter Capaldi's Doctor is trapped for four-and-a-half billion years in a castle trying to break through a wall of Azbantium, a substance harder than diamonds. Though it might take West Ham marginally longer to figure out a way of penetrating the Brighton defence.

We reflect that we really are missing the injured Dawson as we drift disconsolately to The Eagle, where they have a bottle of Abbot in the fridge, at least. Nigel, always one to find statistical comfort in defeat, points out that West Ham are the only team in all four divisions not to have scored a goal this season.

Rather than discuss the game, we mention the possible signing of Emerson and list prog rockers who have played for West Ham, including Felipe (Jon) Anderson and James (Phil) Collins. Nigel is on fine form, revealing that Millwall are the only club to have four of the same letter in their name and that Phil Babb is the only former Premier League star who has a surname with three out of four letters the same. Perhaps he has too much time on his hands.

Three defeats in three league games. We've missed relegation struggles. Is it time to panic? Looking at the game, Brighton had only two shots on target and scored both, but both goals were defensive errors, which can be eliminated. A number of the new signings have not had a proper pre-season and Scamacca, Cornet, Kehrer and Downes are all bedding in, while Aguerd will be back after the December break.

But even so, it's a long time since we've played consistently well, and we've lost the first three games without scoring for only the second time in West Ham's history. The side is looking decidedly jaded after the efforts of the last two seasons. We still have good players but Moyes needs to shake the team up and get something from the now-vital next game at Aston Villa.

The following week sees another new signing. Emerson arrives from Chelsea for £13 million plus £2 million in add-ons – he's hopefully the long-term successor to the nearly 33-year-old Cresswell at left-back. Having got Emerson Palmieri, now all we need to do is sign Lake to keep prog-rock-loving Nigel happy.

I watched Emerson play for Italy against Spain in the 2020 Euros semi-final at Wembley and he looked a decent player.

He also picked up a winners' medal from playing in the final against England. Emerson played twenty-nine times on loan for Lyon last season, but only played thirty-three league games in total for Chelsea, being up against Ben Chilwell and Marcos Alonso. So, at twenty-eight he should still have quite a bit of mileage left in him, and hopefully, he can help us climb up the league.

However, on WhatsApp, Matt feels we could perhaps do with signing another Emerson: 'Our form needs a transcendentalist. Ralph Waldo could provide the self-reliance and experience we need.'

That's seven signings now and on paper, Emerson, Scamacca, Kehrer, Aguerd, Areola, Downes and Cornet are upgrades on departed squad players like Ryan Fredericks, Yarmolenko, Diop, Alex Král and Vlašić. It's going to take time to bed them all in, but surely in the long term results will come, as it's looking like a stronger squad than last season.

There's another Thursday game against Viborg in the Europa Conference League. West Ham's new white and orange away kit will surely have many fans adjusting the contrast controls on their TVs – it looks like a Blackpool kit that has run in the wash.

Soon it's job done in Denmark. It's certainly a great instinctive finish from Scamacca for the first goal when he flicks in Souček's cross. The Irons are indebted to Areola for a fine double save, but the game is made secure with Benrahma's crisp finish into the corner after a fine through ball from Cornet.

Souček bags the third with a good poacher's goal after Lund parries a header. Souček needed a goal more than anyone and, accompanied with an assist, it just might help him see an upturn in form. Though he has at least been getting in scoring positions this season and was unlucky not to net against both Forest and Brighton. There is still time for Cornet to fire over an empty goal after good work by Scamacca and Benrahma.

Credit must go to the noisy Viborg fans, but in the end, it's a satisfying night's work. Scamacca and Cornet benefitted from starting, and it was good to see Ogbonna get another game after his injury and also for Armstrong Oko-Flex to make his Hammers debut. So, it's 3–0 on the night and 6–1 on aggregate. If only we could play Viborg every week.

Three days later, the Irons are back on the Thursday–Sunday treadmill playing at Aston Villa. An article in *The Observer* by Jonathan Wilson wonders if 'David Moyes's bubble is in danger of busting at downbeat West Ham'. Wilson acknowledges that this might be premature, even if West Ham are bottom of the table after three games. But he points out that being a mid-table club in the Premier League is an unforgiving place and that Moyes might not be given the margin for error he had at Everton, even though he consistently got them in the top six. He brings up Moyes's one season at Sunderland that ended in relegation.

Wilson thinks the players are suffering from fatigue and writes that once again, the London Stadium has become 'a pit of grumbles' after vibrant European nights. He takes issue with the move from grafters to more exotic signings: 'These are not players who will necessarily be enthused by the Moyesian grind, and they are perhaps not players he instinctively trusts.'

Wilson, the author of a book on tactics called *Inverting the Pyramid*, goes on to conclude:

> It may be that this is simply the pattern of Everton repeated: Moyesian football can take a limited squad so far, but there is a ceiling – and when results go awry, there is a category of player who will chafe against a tactical approach which, when it is not producing results, can feel restrictive perhaps even to the point of being counterproductive.

At Aston Villa, their manager Steven Gerrard is receiving criticism too, though it does seem pretty early for a must-win game. I receive BBC live updates for the game while on the Ravenglass and Eskdale Railway to Dalegarth in the Lake District, and it makes for happy reading. Emerson starts in a five-man defence, but it's sub Benrahma who changes the performance in the second half as the Irons revert to a back four. Scamacca starts his first game and at least tests Martínez, though he has little service. Aston Villa have a goal correctly disallowed after a corner goes out of play. But finally, the Hammers have some luck late on, when Fornals's shot takes a huge deflection on its way to the top corner. In the end, it's a gritty away win and three welcome points for the Hammers. New signings like Kehrer will gain confidence from keeping a clean sheet. Could this be the start of an upturn?

Moyes tells the BBC, '[We] looked more like ourselves … we were resilient, we stuck at it … The second half we played much better … The Thursday to Sunday stuff can be really difficult … so great credit to the players … We've had two good wins there … so hopefully this is a start and we'll try to push on now.'

A couple of days later, another big signing arrives. Lucas Paquetá has signed from Lyon for a club record fee of £50 million. It's massive money for West Ham and a sign of their new-found ambition. We saw Paquetá play for Lyon in the Europa League last season and he started the move that saw Cresswell sent off in the home leg.

Lisa confides, 'Club record signings make me nervous.'

'No, it's the free ones like Roberto you have to worry about,' replies Fraser, referencing the calamitous keeper signed by Pellegrini.

Paquetá has an impressive record in France and is a regular for Brazil. He looks a Payet-like creative player who could well become a cult figure. Mind you, as some fans might point out, record signings Haller, Anderson, Andy Carroll and Marc-Vivien Foé all had mixed careers with the Hammers. So, let's hope Moyes has done his homework.

August ends with the visit of old adversaries, Spurs. My day begins with a journey from Ravenglass in Cumbria to Euston, after my trip up north Wainwright bagging, and then it's on to the London Stadium with Fraser and Nigel, who has dumped his 'lucky' AFC Wimbledon bag in favour of a 'lucky' Scandinavian Airlines bag and an Ilulissat (it's in Greenland) T-shirt.

Euro-winning Hammer Ellen White is interviewed on the pitch and then the crowd get an introduction to Paquetá. We're joined by Lisa, Matt and Michael, who is carrying an *Anything Goes* programme plus a print-out of his own play. Perhaps he is hoping that he might bump into a theatre impresario in the Billy Bonds Stand.

The game starts at a lively pace, with Ivan Perišić getting in some dangerous crosses and Fornals testing Hugo Lloris with an effort from the edge of the box. Then comes VAR penalty controversy: ref Peter Bankes awards a penalty for handball against Cresswell even though the ball has been played at him from point-blank range. After an interminable VAR delay, the decision is correctly overturned because the ball hit Cresswell on the head and then deflected on to his arm.

The crowd celebrate the overturned penalty as if it's a goal and that inspires West Ham. Rice has a thumping volley punched away by Lloris. Benrahma finds Antonio, who cuts inside and curls an excellent effort against the post.

But Spurs always look threatening on the break, and when Rice advances too far and Benrahma miscontrols the attempted one-two, Spurs burst forward. The pacy Dejan Kulusevski finds the overlapping Kane, who crosses low for Kehrer to poke into his own net under pressure from Son.

The second half starts ominously, as Kulusevski crosses for Son to shoot wide. But the Hammers are starting to press Spurs's defence much more effectively, and Lloris is forced to kick into touch. Coufal's quick throw is controlled by Antonio, who produces a great flick to Souček. Souček has a lot to do but controls well and fires a half-volley into the net to spark pandemonium in the Bobby Moore Stand. That's potato salad to add to Spurs's dodgy lasagne woes. It's a good moment for Antonio, who is in for the ill Scamacca. He's played like a man fighting for his place.

Paquetá comes on in the sixty-seventh minute to make his Hammers debut and immediately looks a skilful addition.

The Irons sense a winner. More pressing sees Souček get a cross in that Bowen pokes wide under pressure. Davinson Sánchez goes close with an overhead kick for Spurs, but the Hammers come again. Coufal is starting to rampage down the right as of old and gets in a decent cross that Fornals volleys over. It's turning into a cracking end-to-end game, as Harry Kane's scuffed volley is dealt with by Fabiański.

Spurs are worried and wasting time. As Pierre-Emile Højbjerg goes down yet again, Mystic Matt suggests that 'there's little more annoying than a self-styled hard man who spends most of their time writhing around pretending to be hurt.'

Can it happen again? Souček wins a lost ball and crosses for Bowen to shoot wide. Then Bowen wins a tackle and races down the right wing to play in the overlapping Souček. Souček gets in an inviting low cross, but subs Paquetá and Emerson leave it to each other.

Right at the end, the ball ricochets off Ogbonna and falls to Bowen, who pokes it agonisingly across goal. The whistle blows, and it's a decent point against a Spurs team tipped to finish in the top six. Once Scamacca and Paquetá are fully integrated then the Hammers can have another good season – this was certainly the best we've played so far.

We retreat to the Refreshment Room for Meantime ale, as Nigel entertains us with interesting facts about Liechtenstein and Matt and Fraser tell us about the times they wound up

Frank Bruno at press conferences. The Hammers deserved to win on chances, but at least this was more like the performances of a year ago. Now West Ham just have to show Chelsea where to stick their blue flag on Saturday. It's been a poor start to the season with a month of transition and the new signings still trying to fit in. But surely the Hammers can now start looking upwards.

2

VAR TROUBLE

SEPTEMBER 2022

September begins with a visit to Chelsea at Stamford Bridge. Paquetá starts his first full match, Fornals is played as an auxiliary left wing back and Benrahma is benched. Poor Beni always seems to get subbed or dropped whenever Moyes wants to keep it tight. A poor first half sees West Ham comfortably contain Chelsea, managed by the soon-to-depart Thomas Tuchel. The second half comes alive when Bowen's excellent full volley is parried by Édouard Mendy for a corner. From the corner, Paquetá gets a head on the cross, which falls to Rice on the left. He plays the ball back into the danger area and Antonio nicks it home from close range in front of the jubilant away fans. Could an upset be on?

But it's hard to ever feel confident at Stamford Bridge, and subs Armando Broja, Kai Havertz and Ben Chilwell make a difference for the Blues. The equaliser comes when Chilwell gets a lucky bounce and swivels to shoot through Fabiański's legs from a tight angle. An alert finish but some hesitant defending, and the keeper should probably have been quicker off his line to block.

But the Hammers keep at it. Sub Benrahma does brilliantly with his cross to give fellow sub Cornet a free header, which he plants against the post. So, it might as well be written that Chelsea will go down the other end and score a late winner. Chilwell gets in a cross from the left and Havertz gets across Ogbonna to score. Should Oggy have been brought on against a top side when he's still getting match fit after a long-term injury? Perhaps Kehrer might have been a bit sharper in the situation.

Yet for once, the Hammers seem to retrieve the game. Under pressure from Bowen, goalkeeper Mendy makes a hash of gathering a back-header and spills the ball to Cornet, who shoots into the roof of the net. Mendy writhes on the ground as if shot by the Grealish Sniper standing on a grassy knoll. Enter sodding VAR, which decides that Bowen's trailing foot has caught Mendy. It's the merest brush with his laces, and Bowen actually jumped over the keeper to avoid clattering him. Moyes gives the officials his Glasgow death stare. How could both the ref Andy Madley and VAR both get this so wrong? Why didn't the ref stick to his decision to award a goal at the monitor?

A point at Stamford Bridge would have been a huge boost. A goal might have kick-started Cornet's Hammers' career too. He only came on the eighty-sixth minute but managed to hit the post and have a goal disallowed. Seasons can turn on decisions like this. Moyes is furious, saying:

> The goalkeeper comes to take it and actually fumbles it out of his hands five or six yards, so he could never recover it. Then he acted as if he had a shoulder injury. I'm amazed that VAR sent the referee for him to see it ... It was a ridiculously bad decision. I'd question VAR as much as the referee, but the referee should have stuck to his own guns today ... there is no excuse for that not to be a goal, none whatsoever. The sad thing is this is the level of the weak refereeing at the moment.

Rice says it's the worst VAR decision ever. Alan Shearer is scathing on *Match of the Day* and says, 'It's as bad a decision as you will ever see.' But none of that will salvage the lost point.

Surely the solution to the ridiculous VAR decisions – and there were several in other games too – is easy. Refs should be trying to reward attacking play with goals rather than looking for pedantic means to disallow them. If there is any grey area at all, the benefit of the doubt should go to the team that has scored. It might also help if the people operating VAR had played the game. There's no way Bowen's challenge was an obvious foul. He tried to avoid Mendy while playing a contact sport, though in the fashion of *Not the Nine O'Clock News*, he might have looked at the keeper in a funny way. If the officials can't agree or it takes more than thirty seconds to decide, then the conclusion should be that there was no offence. Oliver Stone could probably get a whole movie out of this decision. Is it too late for a judicial review? Later in the week, the referees' body – the PGMOL – effectively admits it got the Cornet goal decision wrong.

It might only be four points from five league games, but at least there's the Europa Conference League match against Romanian side FCSB to hopefully boost the players' confidence. Though it's a strange night, as newscasters in black ties have been saying all afternoon that the Queen is seriously unwell. I'm standing by Hackney Wick station at 6.30 p.m. when the news comes through that the Queen has died.

It's too late to postpone the game, though there's a minute's silence at the start plus a spontaneous chorus of 'God Save the Queen' from a large part of the crowd. Queen Elizabeth did open the West Stand at Upton Park, so we might be able to claim her as a Hammer. At half-time, a picture of the Queen handing Bobby Moore the World Cup trophy goes up on the big screens.

It's down to diehards Fraser, Nigel and myself, as Matt and Lisa are called away to reporting duties. The first half sees lots of bouncing away fans. One of the pleasures of the

Conference is the exuberance of the away support. West Ham create chances, but Scamacca still doesn't look sharp after his recent virus and misses West Ham's best chance when set clear by Downes. The Brentwood-born youngster has a decent game, and Emerson looks lively at left-back. But FCSB are dangerous on the break. After failing to score with a free header, they strike with a sweeping move in the thirty-fourth minute as Andrei Cordea fires home.

In a break with precedent, we stay in our seats at half-time and it seems to work, aided again by Nigel's lucky banana. Moyes brings on star names Antonio, Bowen and Paquetá for the second half, and the Irons immediately look better as Antonio troubles the injury-feigning Romanians with his pace. Bowen nets the decisive penalty after Cornet is clattered by the keeper. Paquetá starts to play some incisive through balls and the second goal arrives when the progressive Emerson strokes home after Antonio has forced a save. The third comes after a great turn and shot from Antonio, who has had his best game in ages. Fornals and Antonio almost add more goals.

A strange evening ends, though we're sure the Queen would have been happy to see her beloved West Ham finally beat a Romanian side. Then it's a trip to Hackney Wick in the rain where Nigel meets the West Ham matchday announcer on the Overground, and they bond over stats. Nigel asks which West Ham legend made his debut in the other 3–2 win over Man United (not the win in the final match at the Boleyn). Nigel's answer is Bobby Moore, not that he's a fan of trivia.

Sunday's game against Newcastle is postponed because of the period of royal mourning, so the next outing is seven days later with a Europa Conference away match against Silkeborg in Denmark.

It's the worst possible start after five minutes when Kasper Kusk catches Areola and the defence out with a swift shot from distance. The Hammers are back in it eight minutes later as Lanzini converts his penalty after Cornet is fouled in the box.

As Silkeborg try to play it out of defence, Cornet sets up Scamacca for a thumping shot into the top of the net to put the Irons ahead. Now that was a quality finish. Dawson's header from a corner makes it 3–1 at the break – a good moment for the returning Ballon D'Orson.

But Søren Tengstedt sets up a nervy finish after Bowen loses possession, and Areola parries Tonni Adamsen's shot out to him to make it 3–2. Indeed, it takes a great reflex save from Areola to keep it level as the Danes threaten a late equaliser. But at the whistle, it's a fourth successive victory in the Conference on a tricky night and a welcome return to sporting action.

But it's all very well bossing it in the Europa League. Can the Irons, who are third from bottom after six games, end their poor start to the Premier League season against Frank Lampard's Everton?

The Irons start defensively and seem content to keep it tight until half-time. Bowen has a dangerous cross – well cleared by Conor Coady – early on and a volley over the bar. But Everton take the lead after fifty-three minutes. Neal Maupay, who is completely ineffective for the rest of the season, spins brilliantly to fire in an excellent goal past Fabiański. Rice and Kehrer could perhaps have been tighter on the former Brighton man, who always seems to score against us. Matt comments, 'The Brighton curse is so strong that players take it with them to a new club.' Michael wonders if Moyes will be gone by Christmas.

Demarai Gray fires across the box for the Toffees, but after that the Irons are unlucky. Souček sees a header from a West Ham corner flash across the goal line. An excellent tackle from the Czech then releases substitute Benrahma, who beats reserve keeper Asmir Begović but strikes the inside of the post. Bowen has a goal-bound shot blocked, Cornet has an effort tipped over and only a fine tackle from Nathan Patterson denies Cornet at the death.

So, Everton have their first win of the season and West Ham's poor league start continues with five defeats out of seven games. On WhatsApp, Michael comments, 'I get the feeling it's going to be an unlucky season.'

In *The Guardian*, Jacob Steinberg, a West Ham fan, writes a fair piece pointing out that West Ham have been unlucky but also wondering if the side has gone stale and if Moyes's tactics of 'a low block, plenty of physicality, speedy counterattacks' have been rumbled. He points out that Bowen, who was on fire last season, has not yet scored, Scamacca has only started one league game, Souček looks weary, Coufal has been 'iffy' at right-back, and the side has looked undercooked with the new signings arriving too late to get a good pre-season in.

More crucially, Steinberg wonders if having spent £160 million, Moyes will be afforded time to get the side to gel:

> Expectations have grown. History suggests that David Gold and David Sullivan stick by their managers, but what about Daniel Kretinsky? The Czech billionaire became West Ham's second largest shareholder last November and his arrival has led to greater spending, heightening the suspicion that Moyes could soon be fighting to save his job.

My view is that seven games in, and with four wins in the Europa Conference, there is no need for panic yet. The Hammers would have another point but for the world's worst VAR decision at Chelsea, and playing three of last season's top four in Man City, Spurs and Chelsea in the first seven matches hasn't helped. But there are problems. The Irons have hit the woodwork four times and missed a penalty. Moyes has yet to find an effective attacking combination from Bowen, Antonio, Cornet and Scamacca, while Paquetá is still adjusting to the pace of the Premier League. Though you do get the feeling that when it all clicks, the side might give someone a tonking.

The online critics seem to be forgetting that Moyes has saved West Ham from relegation twice, has then taken the club to sixth and seventh place finishes and has reached the club's first European semi-final since 1976. It's also strange for the moaners to merge the results of two seasons. A slump in the league was always likely towards the end of last season as the small squad tired and the side concentrated on Europe. What matters is this season's results, which haven't been great. But the side isn't getting thrashed every week like Leicester. If we're still in the bottom three after ten games it will be more worrying, but home games against Wolves and Fulham are winnable.

Moyes had a blip season at Everton in 2003–04, finishing seventeenth. But after selling Wayne Rooney, Moyes went on to turn the club around and finish fourth the following season, qualifying for the Champions League. In his last seven seasons at Everton, they always finished in the top eight or higher, twice finishing fifth. So, it seems premature to write him off.

The effort of two near misses at making the top four could

have been demoralising, and some players have probably gone as far as they can with Moyes. He recognised this last season, which is why he has brought in the new signings. He could certainly be more adventurous and try playing Scamacca and Antonio together. But right now, he probably just needs a bit of patience and time to get the new signings performing.

Better news is that Mark Noble has returned to the Irons in the role of sporting director. His retirement could be another reason for the poor start. He has sensibly taken a course at Harvard to learn more about the administrative side of the game, and just his presence around the club will be a boost. Nobes will certainly be a good influence on the younger players and can also help first-team stars adapt to the club culture – last year, Lingard revealed that he was told not to use his mobile by Nobes when the players shared a lift as Mark wanted the squad to talk to each other. He'll also be a sympathetic ear for any players having problems and is closer to their age group.

The two-week international break comes at a good time for West Ham, and now is the time to regroup and bed in the new players. The quality of West Ham's new signings can be seen from the international break. Scamacca almost scores with a header for Italy against England and Emerson makes a late cameo; Kehrer plays at right-back for Germany against

England at Wembley; Areola had a rare outing for France; and Paquetá plays twice for Brazil. Rice also has a solid match for England as he always does. Now is the time for all that international quality to be shown in the Premier League, with two winnable home games coming up.

3

WE'RE ALL GOING ON A EUROPEAN TOUR

OCTOBER 2022

Wolves arrive at the London Stadium for a rare Saturday kick-off, albeit at 5.30 p.m. As a royal tribute, the cover of the programme has a colour picture of a very young-looking Queen in yellow coat and white gloves presenting Bobby Moore with the World Cup in 1966, when the trophy was won by Moore, Geoff Hurst, Martin Peters and eight others. In his manager's notes, Moyes says he hopes the side can rediscover the resilience that has served the team so well in the previous two seasons.

However, a sense of pessimism might be setting in. When Michael asks what the plans are for Saturday, Matt responds, 'Start slowly, concede soft goal, huff and puff, hit the post, make baffling substitutions, have perfectly good goal ruled out by VAR, lose 1–0. Isn't that always the plan?' Michael replies that although he writes scripts, this one is making him feel queasy.

In the Best Cafe, Nigel and Michael join me for a cup of Rosie Lee. Michael's just had his Covid and flu boosters and says he might be away with the fairies, which could be for the best judging by the way the season has gone so far.

Groundhopper Nigel's been to see Oxford City play, and there's no sign of Matt and Lisa, who in a desperate bid to get a mention in my Hammers blog are seeing three games in one day, fitting in the Under-18s and the Under-21s at Rush Green before today's match.

We head off to the match and desperate times require desperate measures: with West Ham in the bottom three, Nigel, in a break from all precedent, opts to eat his lucky banana on the way to the match rather than at half-time. Inside the London Stadium, we meet Fraser and gameaholics Matt and Lisa.

Kehrer is in at right-back for West Ham and Paquetá, Cornet and Scamacca all start. Wolves, who have only scored three goals all season, field a record eight Portuguese players, while gaffer Bruno Lage is forced to play captain Rúben Neves as an emergency central defender.

Results might have been average, but the squad has certainly improved. It's probably the strongest subs bench we've had in the Premier League, consisting of Coufal, Fornals,

Antonio, Lanzini, Areola, Downes, Ogbonna, Benrahma and Emerson. That's a lot of experience and talent, and with that group we have to hope that finally Moyes can make game-changing substitutions. And the Hammers even have a striker on the bench.

Wolves play some neat football in midfield, and early on Fabiański has to make a fairly routine save from a long-range Daniel Podence shot and then a much more difficult save from Jonny. But the Irons slowly come into the game, and Scamacca and Bowen both look in the mood. Cornet heads on, and Scamacca fires just wide from distance.

Bowen runs at the defence and his shot is parried by José Sá, only for Scamacca to send a great chance over the bar. Cornet has to go off injured and is replaced by the hard-working Fornals.

The breakthrough comes after twenty-nine minutes as Scamacca releases Bowen, who runs at the Wolves defence. Bowen's run is blocked by three Wolves defenders but the ball rebounds out to Scamacca on the edge of the box. The Italian takes a touch and fires a thumping half-volley into the corner from outside the box. Now that's a proper goal. Macca needed that first league strike and runs to the fans with an ear-cupping celebration.

At half-time, we have a welcome surprise when we meet returning Irons Steve the Cornish postie and Scott the Clacton Nostradamus (he seemingly predicts 3–2 for every game). There's a scare at the start of the second half as Kehrer clears an innocuous ball straight to Adama Traoré who volleys wide. But minutes later, West Ham get a second goal. Kehrer's shot is blocked but Bowen is alive to the rebound, controlling the ball with his chest and then head as he spins and fires a quick, low shot into the corner. A great finish for his first league goal of the season.

Wolves, without three strikers, have been ineffective in attack, and bringing on former Chelsea striker Diego Costa inspires a chorus of 'Stick your blue flag up your arse...' from the home fans, though the burly Spaniard makes a difference. Costa puts a free header wide and then crosses for Podence to score, though it's correctly disallowed for a marginal offside.

Antonio comes on for Scamacca and is his usual mix of some good pace and control but poor shooting decisions, much to the chagrin of Matt, the vicar's son. But the Hammers hold out. The defence looks a lot better with no-nonsense Dawson in it, a massively underrated player. Zouma has been solid in the air and Kehrer has been quietly effective in our first home win. Moyes will love the clean sheet, and for the first time this season in the league we've scored twice.

All we have to do to ensure another win is for Matt and Lisa to go to three games in a day, Michael to have a Covid jab and Nigel to eat his lucky banana before kick-off. Our change in luck could also be connected with the fact that my lucky 1970s hooped away strip has come out of storage after two months of subsidence work at my gaff. Not that we're superstitious.

We retreat to The Eagle, where there are bottles of Spitfire on offer. As 'Gimme All Your Lovin' plays on the jukebox, our party discusses bands beginning with 'Z', getting ZZ Top, The Zutons and The Zombies, though Michael correctly points out that ZZ Top begins with Zee and not Z. A fight almost starts when Nigel tells Fraser that the West Ham way might be no more and we might have to accept workmanlike wins. It's been a satisfying evening with a vital win, and hopefully the Hammers will soon be looking upwards.

It's two games a week for much of October, and Thursday sees a trip to Anderlecht in the Europa Conference League. The Belgian side are the most difficult opponents in the group and finished third in their league last season. I watch the game at home on BT Sport, while away Irons Matt and Lisa are watching the game in a bar on the Belgian Riviera where they are on a minibreak. They have even found some Cornet Belgian beer. Michael and Fraser report from The Eagle that they now have some proper bitter in the pub fridge just for me.

The Hammers are playing in their non-traditional white and orange away kit. Still, against the side who beat West Ham in the 1976 European Cup Winners' Cup final, it feels like a proper European match with a lively home crowd.

Not too much happens in the first half apart from a late

miss from Benrahma, who scoops over an open goal when set up by a typical driving run and pull-back by Bowen. Saïd has a better low shot saved early in the second half, but a series of Hammers' corners fail to provide a breakthrough and it's left to Moyes to bring on the big three of Rice, Scamacca and Paquetá.

Paquetá looks on form from his first touch – a great pass with the outside of his left boot – and then produces some fine Fancy Dan control on the touchline. The winner comes as Rice plays a crossfield pass to Coufal, who heads back to Paquetá. He dinks a clever ball over the onrushing defender to Scamacca who turns instantly to fire hard and low into the corner. A quality goal all round. West Ham's victory is assured when Areola makes a brilliant one-handed save to deny striker Fábio Silva, who is on loan from Wolves to Anderlecht.

The other big plus of the night is that Downes has a very solid game in midfield and looks like he could provide competition for Souček. Three wins out of three and it's looking increasingly likely we'll be in Europe after Christmas. A lot of fans have been wondering if the distraction of the Europa Conference and the fifteen games it would take to win it is worth it, but on nights like this it feels like a proper competition.

I'm in Barcelona for the Fulham home match, where my sister Pam, who lives in Australia, is taking a cruise back to

Perth. This will be the first home match I miss this season. I'm in the Sagrada Família (designer Antoni Gaudí quite possibly based it upon Nigel's lucky banana to judge by the fruit motifs on this extraordinary building) as the news comes through on WhatsApp that West Ham have beaten Fulham 3–1. Messages from my West Ham group reveal that The Eagle has Spitfire in stock but strangely no Basqueland IPA or tapas.

Later, I find *Match of the Day* on the hotel TV. West Ham have a dodgy start, with Andreas Pereira lashing home from a tight angle after Zouma fails to close him down in the box. It's a rasping shot, but should Fabiański have got his hands up quicker? It's nearly 2–0 after Dan James hits the bar with a thumping shot.

But at the other end, Paquetá is starting to find pockets of space and establish a partnership with Scamacca. He creates three great chances for the Italian, crossing for Scamacca to force a great save from Bernd Leno with a header, then playing a through ball which the Italian strokes wide. Paquetá then creates another headed opportunity for Scamacca as he plays it out from the back for Cresswell to cross. I wonder what the Italian for barn door is.

The breakthrough comes after Rice feeds Paquetá. He finds Cresswell with a great ball out of defence and West Ham force a corner. Despite three warnings from the ref, Pereira takes Dawson out with an American football-style block to concede a stupid penalty. Bowen does the rest, and credit to Dawson for so unsettling the Cottagers' defence. It's no coincidence that West Ham's form has improved at both ends since Ballon D'Orson returned.

The second half sees West Ham take the lead as Paquetá dinks the ball through to Scamacca, who delicately lobs the keeper. He doesn't celebrate, fearing a VAR call for offside or handball. The ball bounced up against Scamacca's elbow as he controlled it. After a long VAR debate, the goal is given as it's inconclusive whether the ball had also brushed the striker's fingers. That's Scamacca's sixth goal of the season, and like all quality marksmen, he's kept going even when he's missed a few.

Cresswell has to block Tom Cairney's goal-bound shot but at the death, substitute Antonio wraps it up. It's a bit of a comedy goal. Micky uses his strength to get past the Fulham defence, then fires straight at Leno, which turns into a one-two off the keeper. Leno and Tim Ream then get in a terrible muddle as the defender prods the ball against his own keeper, and Antonio keeps calm to sidestep them both and tap the ball into the net. There's also been an inadvertent handball by Antonio in the build-up, but it was in the first phase of the attack, and we'll take whatever VAR luck we can get after the debacle of Cornet's disallowed goal at Chelsea.

That's three wins in a row and three in three for Scamacca. The biggest plus is that Paquetá is now looking like the playmaker West Ham have needed. For too long the side has relied on Rice and Bowen, so adding Paquetá to the mix can only help.

After the match, Fulham manager Marco Silva has a big and perhaps understandable sulk, refusing to talk about the referee for fear of suspension: 'I will not say to you what I think … until the penalty we were clearly the best team on the pitch.' Moyes says he thought West Ham deserved the win after a slow start and are 'going in the right direction'. It was a 'stonewall penalty' says Moyesy, adding that he 'really enjoyed bits of the play'.

It's two games a week for ever, it seems. You need stamina to be a West Ham fan. It's another Thursday nighter and the big news at the London Stadium is that Nigel and Gav (Nigel's old school friend from Brentwood) have been to see Uriah Heep last week and are seeing Deep Purple on Thursday, though Lisa would prefer Bucks Fizz. Meanwhile, Nigel has eaten his lucky banana in the tunnel by Carpenters Road rather than at half-time, a tactic that has resulted in three wins in a row.

It's a noisy midweek crowd as the Hammers soon go two goals up. Benrahma curls a fine free kick through the Anderlecht wall (Matt has never doubted him), and then after a good run by Emerson, Bowen lashes home from the edge of the box. Anderlecht have some late chances but it's 2–0 at the interval, with an injury to Ogbonna the only downside.

There's a medical drama at half-time as an unfortunate fan falls down the steps in the Billy Bonds Stand. The paramedics do a professional job, and the supporter is eventually taken away on a stretcher with his neck in a brace and his arm in a sling.

In the second half, the Irons continue to miss chances, and Fornals and sub Souček should both do better with their opportunities. Meanwhile, the away fans have been setting off flares all game and there are unpleasant scenes as seats are thrown and flares thrown at West Ham fans. 'Some stupid with a flare gun could burn this place to the ground,' opines Nigel, channelling Deep Purple's 'Smoke on the Water'.

When Anderlecht score a late penalty, which is given even though Johnson seemed to play the ball, more flares are lobbed. 'Eddie and the Hot Rods once wrote a song about fighting Belgians,' says Nigel – always happy to provide niche musical information – referring to 'Ignore Them (Always Crashing in the Same Bar)'.

A shame about the crowd trouble but at the end of the evening it's job done as the Irons make it four out of four wins in Europe. A good result considering Moyes made seven changes – and more importantly, this ensures European football after Christmas, which doesn't happen often at West Ham.

By the time the Sunday match at Southampton arrives,

I have contracted Covid and feel about as well as a winger trying to skip past Julian Dicks. I listen on Radio London while laid up in bed.

Emerson goes close early on after good work by Scamacca, but the Saints come back with Fabiański saving with his feet from Che Adams. The home side take the lead as, bizarrely, the referee obstructs Bowen, preventing him tackling Romain Perraud who fires home a deflected shot.

Fabiański has to make a brilliant low save from Adams, but the response from the Irons is good as Scamacca fires two efforts just wide and then crosses for Paquetá to head against the outside of the post.

The second half is all West Ham as the Irons force numerous corners. Sub Benrahma makes a difference and should surely be started more regularly. On the left, Rice plays a swift one-two with Benrahma and curls a lovely shot into the far corner for his first league goal in a year, topped off by a knee-slide celebration in front of the away fans. Scamacca has an effort saved late on and Benrahma has a goal-bound shot blocked, but the determined Saints hold on for a point.

The worrying thing is that the Hammers couldn't win with 61 per cent possession, twenty-five shots and fourteen corners. Perhaps the injured Dawson and Zouma might have made a difference at set-pieces. Still, it was a decent performance overall in terms of chances made, and surely the goals will come. Moyes also reckons we should have had a penalty for a foul on Souček and *Match of the Day 2* does indeed reveal a judo throw on him by Perraud.

The relentless run of league matches continues with an away match at Anfield on Wednesday as the fixtures are squeezed in to provide space for the sportswashing World Cup in December.

It's a blow that Paquetá misses the game with a shoulder injury. Moyes opts to go with Downes as a third holding midfielder, which looks over-cautious to most fans. It begins as the Darwin Núñez show, with the striker forcing a great save from Fabiański with a stunning half-volley. Núñez then powerfully heads home Konstantinos Tsimikas's cross for the opener and forces another good save from Fabiański. As if that's not enough, he strikes the post with another volley, and the Irons seem to be losing the Darwinian survival battle.

Another thrashing at Anfield? Maybe not. Shortly before the break, the under-pressure Irons have a chance to come back into it. Downes's knock-on to Bowen sees the forward barged over by Joe Gomez and after some VAR debate, a penalty is awarded. But Bowen never looks that confident taking it in front of the Kop and Alisson Becker pulls off an athletic save. It's not that bad a penalty, but since Noble retired, finding a penalty taker has been a problem and that's two missed this season. Perhaps, unlike Liz Truss's ill-fated budget, we need to get an assessment from the Office for Penalty-Taking

Responsibility. Soon after the save, Kehrer goes close with a header from a corner.

After the break, Liverpool create more chances and Zouma almost scores an own goal. But subs Benrahma and Antonio cause problems as Moyes finally plays Antonio and Scamacca together, albeit briefly. Scamacca shoots wastefully wide when set up by Antonio with Benrahma free in the middle. Benrahma doesn't connect properly with his volley after Rice's dropping cross falls at his feet. Then, after great work from Benrahma and Bowen on the left Souček looks certain to score, only to be robbed by a great tackle from James Milner and a deflection off Alisson.

So, it's another defeat. In recent seasons, West Ham seem to have perfected the art of losing unluckily at Anfield. At some stage the Irons have to start taking chances against the big teams away, although this was a decent performance and at times, one of the best teams in Europe were worried. Youngsters like Downes and Scamacca will have learned from playing here, at least.

The day after the Liverpool defeat, Prime Minister Liz Truss resigns, having crashed the economy and spooked the markets. Her 45-day reign has been like some of West Ham's worst moments: a new owner or gaffer coming in and promising endless growth only to find we are bottom of the table. On WhatsApp, Lisa wonders if Big Sam is available to save the UK from relegation. We also suggest Harry Redknapp, who could maybe arrange a few swap deals with the SNP. Eventually, the job of keeping Britain up goes to Rishi Sunak.

The Bournemouth game is a Monday night fixture on Sky. At the London Stadium, Michael the Whovian has been watching 'The Power of the Doctor' the previous evening and Nigel has forgotten to eat his lucky banana but is still dreaming of being a 'Highway Star' after seeing the superannuated Deep Purple. Fraser is liking the Tory idea of replacing the gaffer every six weeks. Matt and Lisa complete our party on a rare day of only going to one match.

It is a bit of a strange selection by Moyes. Downes is played in Paquetá's number ten role rather than as a holding midfielder, which would allow Rice and Souček to get forward. But the Hammers dominate most of the first half against ex-Hammer Gary O'Neil's men, going close first with a Souček header. After a Downes shot is blocked, Cresswell draws a great save from Neto. At the other end, Souček gives the ball away and allows Dominic Solanke to get a shot in.

Bowen isn't really getting into the game and Scamacca is outnumbered and not using his 6ft 5in. frame to good effect. Benrahma is a threat on the left and even though he makes a few rickets, he always wants the ball. The breakthrough comes from a corner just before the break. It's an ugly goal, but we'll take it. The ball strikes Kehrer on the arms, Souček heads it back in and Zouma gets a flick to head it home. VAR gives it despite Kehrer's handball, as it is deemed not deliberate and in the phase of play before the goal is scored. You can always rely on Mike Dean at Stockley Park.

Meanwhile, Mystic Matt has to delete his half-time tweet criticising Bournemouth's play-acting as both Solanke and keeper Neto go off with genuine injuries. If there's an actual severed leg, he might consider an injury genuine.

The second half sees Rice have a shot saved by substitute keeper Mark Travers, but then the Hammers slowly let Bournemouth into the game. Downes fades in his attacking role and Johnson has a bit of a nightmare at right-back, while Scamacca tries to take on one man too many. Benrahma is the best outlet, at times showing great control and having shots from all angles.

Ex-Hammer Ryan Fredericks gets a good round of applause from the home fans when he goes off. Antonio comes on for Scamacca, throws himself to the ground a lot and doesn't hold it up very well, in a much less effective cameo than William Russell, Sophie Aldred, Janet Fielding and David Tennant made in *Doctor Who* last night. Nigel remarks that 'it seems a long time ago when we were playing well and in the top four'.

Moyes doesn't make any further changes until the eighty-eighth minute, bringing on Coufal and Fornals as the Hammers defend their one-goal lead. We're into the ninetieth minute as Coufal gets in a cross that the diving Jordan Zemura blocks with his hand. It's hard to see how the defender could have got out of the way but according to the letter of the law and Mike Dean, it's a penalty. The newly blond Benrahma smashes it home in emphatic style. Have we finally found our penalty taker?

There's much shock when Matt says he is giving the man of the match award to Benrahma – having obviously never doubted him. From flirting with the bottom three, West Ham go up to tenth in the congested Premier League. The Irons deserved to win on possession, though they have had to rely on a couple of contentious VAR calls – still, that's an impressive five home wins in a row, the first time the Hammers have done this since the move from the Boleyn Ground six years ago.

Our party heads to Ye Olde Black Bull, which is serving Tribute and Wherry, and sensibly declines to discuss emotions, instead sticking to trivia. We go through Scottish islands, major UK towns Nigel hasn't been to (Dundee take a bow) and MPs without a football team in their constituency. It's left to Nigel to come up with some absolutely world-class trivia: Benrahma has scored three goals this season all under different Prime Ministers, Boris Johnson, Liz Truss and Rishi Sunak. Matt quips, 'Antonio's last three goals have come under seventy-two Prime Ministers, stretching back to Lord Liverpool.' The performance has been underwhelming, but a win is a win, and surely the team can start looking upwards.

Three days later, the side is in action again against Silkeborg in the Europa Conference. Most of us have booked late, and despite the strange ticket office practise of not selling tickets next to an empty single seat, Matt, Lisa, Fraser, Nigel and I are able to find enough wide open spaces to sit together in our usual spot. The evening begins with the usual European fanfare of epic music, flame throwers on the pitch and a mass display of red and white scarves from the Silkeborg fans – who seem a much friendlier bunch than the Belgians of Anderlecht with their flares and seat lobbing.

Antonio goes close early on, shooting at the keeper's leg after a fine through ball from Fornals. It's good to see Nayef Aguerd finally make his debut and he looks an assured presence with a cultured left foot. It's a good run-out for him against a side that looks about Championship standard.

The Irons continue to press, with Benrahma setting up Coventry for a shot just past the post. The only goal comes after half an hour. The ball appears to be drifting off, but keeper Nicolai Larsen foolishly rushes off his line and Antonio goes down like a felled tree after some slight contact. It's a very soft penalty, but Lanzini dispatches it, even though the keeper gets close.

The second half sees Fornals drag a great chance wide after a defender passes straight to him. But slowly, West Ham's B team start to ease off, and Anders Klynge tests Areola with a low effort. The West Ham keeper then has to make a great leap to defy Tengstedt. Are we about to be assimilated by the Borg?

At the other end, it's almost two goals as Benrahma cuts inside from a corner only to see Larsen's foot deflect the ball wide. Moyes plays Antonio and Scamacca together for a whole sixteen minutes, while Rice and Souček are brought on late to shore it up. We should have had more, but a team of squad players has done a professional job.

We head off to Ye Olde Black Bull for some pints of Razor Back, where Fraser says there's nothing he enjoys more than a clean sheet and a 1–0 victory through a dodgy penalty. Nigel's hoping that Barrow versus Crewe will be a better game, where he'll complete his ninety-two grounds aided by groundhopper Reg. And inspired by Conor Coventry, he's wondering if any players have played for a club with the same surname – and thinks we should loan Coventry to Coventry just to make it happen. On WhatsApp, the absent Michael asks in disbelief if Antonio and Scamacca really played together for ten minutes. Matt replies that it is 'the most dysfunctional relationship since Prince Charles and Lady Diana'.

That's six home wins in a row now, even if three were in the Europa Conference. West Ham have won the group, the kids can now play against FCSB and it's European football again in March. That's not a bad achievement at all.

A difficult away game at Man United ends the month. It's

another negative team selection from Moyes for a big away game, with Paquetá still injured and three defensive midfielders starting. Downes is a promising holding midfielder but he plays virtually every ball backwards to Rice – playing Downes in the number ten role seems bizarre when Antonio, Fornals or Lanzini would be a much better fit.

The first thirty-seven minutes see United restricted to a couple of efforts from Ronaldo and Marcus Rashford, both comfortably dealt with by Fabiański. Benrahma almost gets through on a couple of occasions but it's generally unambitious fare from the Hammers, who again seem to be playing in Blackpool's discarded kit. United's goal arrives when Christian Eriksen collects a throw-in and spins in a lovely cross for the resurgent Rashford to get above right-back Kehrer and power home a header.

Areola has to come on for the injured Fabiański as the Hammers struggle. Scamacca isn't doing it in the big games. After picking up a silly booking and then making a rash challenge, he's taken off for his own protection. Substitute Antonio makes a difference with his hold-up play, and for the final half an hour the Hammers give it a real go. Diogo Dalot has to make a great defensive header to thwart Antonio, and then Micky tests David de Gea with a long-range piledriver, forcing a brilliant save.

De Gea produces a great flying save to deny Zouma, who has got his head on Cresswell's cross. Fred heads against the post at the other end, but still West Ham come forward. Fornals, on for Downes, does really well to pull the ball back, only for Bowen's goal-bound shot to be deflected wide by Harry Maguire.

In the last action of the day, Benrahma's run causes panic and Rice sends in a hypersonic missile of a shot that de Gea somehow tips wide. West Ham really should have got a point from this and you have to hope that at some point the team's luck will turn in front of goal. De Gea always seems to reserve his best form for the Hammers.

Moyes says the side deserved something. The Irons seem to have perfected the art of losing unluckily by one goal to the top six clubs. That's unlucky one-goal defeats at Chelsea, Liverpool and United. At least we have the chance to get some revenge at the London Stadium after the World Cup. And to be positive, Antonio had a good game as a pundit on *Match of the Day 2*, giving some personable analysis. It's not a time for panic, but Moyes needs to restore some adventure, get Paquetá fit and find a result in the next home game against Palace.

4

WE'RE LOSING AT HOME

NOVEMBER 2022

The Hammers, having already topped their group, are able to field a side of youngsters and squad players at FCSB in a Europa Conference League dead rubber. There are two academy debutants in sixteen-year-old Ollie Scarles and eighteen-year-old striker Divin Mubama. Scarles gets in some great crosses. Striker Mubama, who might prove to be a younger version of Antonio, is a handful all evening and nearly scores from Scarles's cross in the first few minutes.

The Hammers take the lead when Johnson's long ball is expertly finished by Fornals on the half-volley. The Hammers' second goal appears to have been headed home by young Mubama from Coufal's cross, though it proves to have taken a deflection off Joyskim Dawa and is deemed an own goal. The third comes when another excellent cross from Scarles is fumbled by the keeper and Fornals lashes home. More of that in the Premier League please, Pablo.

Scarles almost strokes home a fourth, but he shoots just wide. But overall, it is a very satisfying evening and another game for Aguerd to gain match fitness in. The other bonus is late substitute debuts for Kaelan Casey, Kamarai Simon-Swyer, Keenan Appiah-Forson and Freddie Potts.

Then it's back to the more pressing matter of league points. West Ham have three home games in a week coming up. Crystal Palace at the London Stadium appears to be a winnable game.

It has rained all morning, and the Overground is down yet again so it's not a promising start to my Sunday. Inside the stadium are Fraser in his Humphrey Bogart raincoat, Matt wearing a yellow hoodie (is he now a Watford fan?), Lisa, Michael and Nigel, fresh from recompleting his ninety-two league grounds at exotic Barrow in a road trip with his pal Reg.

Up against a team that hasn't won away all season – what could possibly go wrong? Palace have much the better of the first nineteen minutes, as Eberechi Eze tests Fabiański with a free kick and then drags a good chance wide. Eze, Wilfried Zaha, Michael Olise and Jordan Ayew are a fluid attack for Palace while West Ham look strangely jaded, despite having rested the senior players on Thursday.

But slowly, West Ham get into the game more and take a

surprise lead. Paquetá finds Benrahma with a short ball and the Algerian sidesteps a defender to send a rocket into the top corner. That's a great goal.

It looks like the Hammers will take the lead into the break until an unforced error. Fabiański rolls the ball out to Dawson, whose overhit pass is miscontrolled by Kehrer. Eze pounces and sets up Zaha for a crisp finish.

Scamacca has played a few decent balls out wide but has generally struggled to hold the ball up in the first half and is replaced by Antonio at the break. Scamacca still seems to be adapting to the Premier League and his form has slumped in recent weeks, which is worrying.

The Irons improve a bit, but quite often the passing is woeful. When the lively Benrahma is subbed by Lanzini, there's a dissenting chant of 'Oh Saïd Benrahma!' Moyes later reveals that Benrahma was carrying a knee injury but also adds that he didn't think Benrahma did much after his goal – we think Moyes really needs to stop digging him out, as he's clearly a confidence player. The substitution of the previously untouchable Souček for Downes gets ironic cheers.

Antonio is struggling to hold it up, just as Scamacca did, but causes problems with his strength. When Lanzini finds Antonio, he loses his defender with a great turn, nears the goalkeeper and then rather than shoot or pass to Paquetá, falls to the ground. The ref gives a penalty, only for VAR to correctly overturn it.

'Why can you not pass it?!' asks Matt, the increasingly incensed vicar's son, as the Hammers continue to lose possession, with Bowen working hard but toiling and the Hammers missing Coufal's attacking runs. Dawson almost turns the ball into his own net but is saved by Fabiański. A great tackle from Dawson then denies Zaha. Have both sides now settled for a draw?

With four minutes of added time, West Ham stream forward in search of a late winner that would boost our season. Antonio bounces off a defender and races into the right side of the box. He could fire it hard and low to try and get a deflection or a corner. Or just waste some time. But instead, he lofts a feeble chip into the arms of Vicente Guaita.

The next fifteen seconds seem preordained. Guaita plays it out, Eze finds Olise and the Palace winger's shot takes a wicked deflection off Cresswell to fly into the top corner with the last kick of the game. The Palace fans go wild, while we feel bad all over. The big screen scoreboard reads 'WHU 1 CRY 2', which seems very apt.

At least The Eagle has bottles of Spitfire in the fridge as we resort to drink and watch Spurs versus Liverpool. Nigel tells us about the sights of Barrow, Matt recalls Terry Pratchett stories and Michael pumps us for information on *Stranger Things* as he has to review a play based on it – which, being a TV series about kids in an upside-down world, sounds curiously like West Ham. And like Kate Bush, we do seem to be always 'Running Up That Hill'. Moyes tells the media 'we shot ourselves in the foot', prompting Matt to quip that 'it's surprising we didn't miss'.

The midweek Carabao Cup game against Blackburn offers hope of getting back on track. In the Best Cafe, Michael has purchased an unusual gift for Nigel – a plastic banana case for his lucky banana. This novelty item is yellow, banana-shaped and comes with a fork. We're joined by Matt and Lisa who, taking advantage of the Best's evening menu, are quaffing red wine in the style of Malcolm Allison, whom Matt once spotted with a bottle of plonk in the Central pub. The Best's daytime greasy spoon menu is off so it's falafel and chips all round.

Somehow, Nigel gets his rigid banana case past security despite it being an offensive weapon, and we join Fraser in the stadium. As ever, the Irons start slowly against Blackburn's second eleven and a back pass from Aguerd almost gifts Rovers the lead. Rovers score after six minutes as Jack Vale gets behind the home defence to stroke home. Oh dear.

Our mainly squad players need to raise their game. The League Cup is, after all, one of our best chances of winning a trophy. Antonio starts to cause a few problems, dribbling down the left to cross low for Fornals to fire at the keeper. The same pair manage to fashion an equaliser. Antonio's run from the right causes confusion and his cross is miscontrolled by a defender into the path of Fornals, who finishes crisply for his third goal in a week.

After the break, a terrible back pass by Coventry almost gifts Blackburn a second goal, though Aguerd does well to block on the line. Lanzini has a goal-bound shot blocked, but then sub Benrahma gives the side an instant lift. He sets up a chance for Antonio to fire at the keeper, only for Benrahma to then blast the rebound over the bar.

Moyes brings on Scamacca and Bowen to support Antonio and Benrahma in a bid to settle the tie. Antonio hits the post from a corner. Aguerd plays a long ball into the box, a Blackburn defender gets a boot in ahead of Bowen and Antonio lashes home the loose ball to make it 2–1 with twelve minutes left. Surely, it's the winner?

But the Hammers have not heeded the threat of substitute and rumoured West Ham target Brereton Díaz, who has already cut in from the left and fired wide. After a poor free kick straight into the arms of Aynsley Pears, Rovers break, and Díaz is given too much time by Johnson and Aguerd to cut in and fire into the top corner. A great goal but very poor defensively.

So, the tie goes down to penalties, which are surprisingly well taken. Areola doesn't get close to any of them, however, and nor does Rovers' Pears. Benrahma, Bowen, Scamacca, Antonio and Lanzini score the first five, as do Blackburn, and then it's sudden death. When it reaches 10–9, Ogbonna steps up to fire against the bar and send Blackburn through to the next round. 'How shit must you be, our first team's at home!' chant the delighted Rovers fans.

'We won't ever see a Moyes team score eleven again,' reflects Fraser. Nigel's lucky banana case has failed to work any magic, though it has resulted in a 23-goal thriller. But we're out of the League Cup, which was a good chance of a trophy. Elimination might help avoid fixture congestion if there is a Europa Conference run, but even so, it piles pressure on Moyes to get a result in the Leicester game, though he certainly deserves time to reset the squad during the World Cup break.

Inspired by a half-time meeting with Nigel's old school pal Gavin, who is sporting a 1970s Middlesbrough away shirt – as you do if you are a great collector of footballing memorabilia – we head to a bar above a Chinese restaurant in Westfield. Meantime ale is available at £6 a pint, though the soft lighting gives the place a distinct 1970s James Bond vibe, which rather like West Ham leaves us shaken but not stirred. Had we won the shoot-out this might have been regarded as fairly routine progress, but we didn't and the slow starts and the defensive lapses are becoming increasingly worrying.

The strangest news for the Leicester match is that it's taking place at 3 p.m. on a Saturday. Surely this goes against all football tradition? West Ham play on Sundays, Mondays,

Tuesdays, Wednesdays, Thursdays and Fridays at all hours but never on a Saturday. We can't see this Saturday football business catching on. This is the last game of the mini-season before the World Cup starts, so a win would certainly help the side's confidence.

In the Best Cafe, Matt is quizzing us on the nine current and past West Ham players likely to be going to the World Cup. He's particularly pleased that we don't get Edimilson Fernandes of Switzerland and Javier Hernández of Mexico, though we do guess Cheikhou Kouyaté of Senegal.

At the match, the sun is in our eyes despite the promises of the man at the reservation office six years ago when West Ham moved stadiums. At first, we think the Cockney Rejects have mellowed and got a brass section, though the band on the pitch prove to be here for Remembrance Sunday and do a nice version of 'Bubbles', which brings back memories of the old 1970s brass band.

West Ham start with some attacks for a change but still go behind after eight minutes. Kehrer jockeys Harvey Barnes away from goal but Paquetá hasn't tracked Kiernan Dewsbury-Hall, who crosses for Patson Daka. The Leicester striker miskicks, but it falls to James Maddison, who is more alert than Cresswell and fires into the roof of the net.

Fabiański has to make a great save from a long-distance shot from Daniel Amartey, while Zouma, who pulled up in the warm-up, has to go off to be replaced by Aguerd. Faced with adversity, the Irons make a spirited response, helped by Maddison departing with an injury. Benrahma does really well to wriggle through and force a one-handed save from Danny Ward. The Leicester keeper then makes another fine save after Paquetá's header is looping into the top corner, and Souček has a goal disallowed for offside.

But the Hammers then crumble at the back again. Dawson tackles through Daka before getting the ball, and though the ref rules play on, VAR decides, correctly for once, that it's a penalty. Thankfully, Fabiański makes a great save to keep out Youri Tielemans's well-struck spot-kick.

Nigel's lucky banana and new banana case still aren't working, not that we rely on bizarre superstitions and a belief in mystical fruit to ensure success. The second half sees West Ham produce one of their better performances of the season, only to lack any kind of clinical finish. Kehrer gets in a fine cross, but Scamacca hasn't gambled to get on the end of it. Rice puts a free header over the bar and shoots wide. A series of corners come to nothing as Moyes replaces Souček with Fornals. Rice is everywhere but we miss the crossing ability of Coufal. Bowen, who looks tired and is often too deep, has one shot deflected over and is then foiled by a great block as Wout Faes and the Leicester defence excel.

The game is sealed with twelve minutes to go as Ayoze Pérez plays in Barnes, who gets past Aguerd too easily and slips the ball past the onrushing Fabiański. Worryingly, West

Ham heads go down even though the match is still redeemable. Leicester see the game out comfortably. West Ham head into the World Cup hiatus sitting in sixteenth place, one point above the relegation zone.

It's off to The Eagle for our last drink until after Christmas. Three home games and three defeats in six days – it doesn't get worse than this. Moyes has done a great job in the last two seasons, but his project has undoubtedly stalled. He deserves time over the break to try to get Paquetá, Scamacca, Kehrer, Aguerd and the injured Cornet playing in a united team, but it's all looking disjointed, and the side needs the elusive elixir of confidence. European progress has been excellent, but having spent big, the Hammers have to be better than this otherwise a relegation struggle beckons.

After the game, Moyes says:

> We played well … I thought we played well for good periods of the game today. We couldn't turn the good periods into goals … People are … more used to being sixth or seventh in the league.

With relatively few players at the World Cup and a break of six weeks, it's now a chance for Moyes and his staff to work hard on the training ground and look at resetting the team. Perhaps the biggest issue is that other teams seem to have rumbled how to play against West Ham. Sitting deep and breaking at speed has worked in the previous two and a half seasons, but it hasn't been effective this season, and the policy of sitting back for the first half of away games usually leads to the team going a goal down. It's surely time to be more proactive away from home.

There are a number of issues for Moyes to ponder. Can Antonio and Scamacca play together up front? Yes, it would mean depleting the midfield, but Antonio could easily play wide right and get forward in support of Macca when necessary. Though Moyes is unlikely to change from his single striker default position. And how do West Ham build a team around Paquetá? We need to get the £50 million midfielder on the ball and in positions where he can really affect games. Too often his fancy backheels and close control are done in areas where he doesn't hurt the opposition.

Right-back has also been a problem position, which has been shared between Johnson, Kehrer and Coufal. Kehrer looks more at home as a centre-back, while Johnson's form has declined, and he sometimes looks unsure going forward. My preference would be for playing Coufal for his crossing prowess and work ethic, in the hope he can get back to the levels of two seasons ago.

Set-pieces have also declined. Despite a lot of height in the side, the Irons have hardly scored from a set-piece, with just

Zouma's goal against Bournemouth coming from a corner. Dawson used to cause mayhem, Ogbonna was a threat and Souček used to score his fair share of headers. The departed Stuart Pearce did a lot of work on set-pieces and it's something the management now need to work on. And we never seem to score in the first half anymore.

Benrahma has probably been the Hammers' best player so far. But surely Moyes needs to be less harsh on him and give him more confidence with the arm-round-the-shoulder approach, rather than qualifying every statement with a criticism.

And then there's Bowen. Last season he was on fire and dating Dani Dyer. But playing for England at the end of the season did his body no favours and he's looked jaded. Perhaps he's been trying too hard to get into Gareth Southgate's World Cup squad. He should benefit from a six-week rest. Bowen needs to have his confidence boosted by the management and be encouraged to get his shots away as of old. Apart from these issues, everything has been going well.

Still, a better farewell to the mini-season is held at the Newham Bookshop on the Sunday after the Leicester defeat. Mark Noble is signing copies of *Boleyn Boy*, his new autobiography, written with *The Guardian*'s Jacob Steinberg.

The Newham Bookshop in Barking Road is the best independent bookshop in London and was an Upton Park pre-match institution for fans like myself until the club moved to Stratford in 2016. My daughters used to love its extensive children's section, and there are even cups of tea offered to favoured clients. The shop has continued to flourish despite West Ham leaving, thanks to its great service and strong links with the local community. Manager Vivian Archer, who was once an actor and appeared in *Z-Cars*, has been in charge for thirty-five years and can find whatever you want among the teetering piles of books, which give it a pleasingly Dickensian feel.

The bookshop has also hosted numerous West Ham signings. Meeting Trevor Brooking signing his book there was a personal highlight, and other West Ham-associated writers to host events there include John Lyall, Geoff Hurst, Martin Peters, Julian Dicks, Frank McAvennie, Tony Gale, Danny Dyer, Steve Bacon, Brian Williams, Jeremy Nicholas, Robert Banks, Iain Dale, Cass Pennant, Tina Moore and Brian Belton. I've even done a few book signings there myself.

For Noble's signing session, the queues of fans stretch round the block and the shop has sold all of the 400 copies it has in stock. Demand is so great Noble even has to fetch twenty copies from his car boot. Vivian tells me the queue started at 9 a.m. and one Hammers fan has travelled all the way up from Dorset.

Vivian has employed me as an assistant for some reason,

marshalling the queue and standing behind Noble's signing table like a cross between a minder and a pen carrier. I even get to hand the West Ham legend a copy of my own book, *Goodbye to Boleyn*.

Nobes is obviously very impressed to meet local legend Vivian and as ever, proves to be a diamond geezer. He has a word for everyone during his two-hour session and is great with kids and starstruck fans alike. 'He seems to think I was called "geez",' deadpans Fraser. Indeed, Nobes employs the simple PR expedient of calling all the blokes 'geez' and the women 'darlin'.

My daughter Lola is down from Edinburgh and gets a little starstruck talking to Mark as he signs her book. He calls Matt a 'geez' too as he signs a Christmas present for Lisa and also signs copies for uber-geezers Michael and Fraser.

Through earwigging as Noble meets the punters, I learn that Benrahma is fantastic in training, the most stressful thing about retirement is 'watching West Ham' and that Noble likes a Bounty bar, as his two sons are dispatched to the car to get some chocolate. Top man and as many fans have said, we could do with him on the pitch now.

The book itself, rather like its subject, puts in a no-nonsense shift. Mark got up to a few tricks as a kid, paying £5 to his mate on a burger stall at the ground and receiving £20 in change. He was also briefly tempted by hooliganism but after seeing a ruck with Millwall fans decided it was all a bit too scary. From a young age, he knew he was a bit special at football, and with a lot of support from his dad, turned down approaches from Arsenal and Millwall and opted for the Irons. Another rock in his life is his girlfriend and now-wife, Carly.

Nobes has some interesting thoughts on his managers, not least the revelation that the players tried to talk Gianfranco Zola into making a comeback as a player. He respected Sam Allardyce and seems to agree with Big Sam that the West Ham Way is more about showing you care than pretty football.

Nobes feels Dimitri Payet should have spoken to his skipper first about his homesickness but says that Dimi still 'made my life as West Ham captain so beautiful for eighteen months'. There is also a section about the players' japes, and you probably don't want to know what Robert Snodgrass did with Nobes's slippers.

Noble's take on removing that pitch invader against Burnley is interesting:

> It was my way of saying, 'Look, I'm a fucking West Ham fan. I've supported the team since I was born. But you don't run on the field of play.' I was as frustrated as anyone. I trained hard every day and hurt when we lost. Yet it's not fair to affect the game and disturb the players.

That evening he went home and when Carly brought him a cup of tea, he burst into tears at the state of the club. He writes that he has a lot of respect for Moyes and praises his decision to take the players on a break after that Burnley debacle.

Reading *Boleyn Boy*, you get a sense of how difficult it has been at times being both a West Ham fan and a player, but Noble has certainly earned our affection. Having him back at the club can only be a good thing.

After the signing, we have a coffee opposite the statue of Moore, Hurst and Peters on Barking Road. The big news is that Fraser, following pancreatic problems, has been advised to give up alcohol. Not drinking will surely test any West Ham fan, particularly one who longs for the days of Greenwood and Lyall.

We walk back to Upton Park tube station. It's sad to see the old Boleyn Ground, which is now a series of square housing blocks, although there is a Lyall House. Ken's Cafe is now a burger bar, which is very sad, and Ken has passed on to the great kitchen above. However, the Boleyn Tavern has definitely improved now the sticky carpet has gone and the Victorian fixtures and fittings have been highlighted. It's a rather swish gastro pub with a fine selection of beers, unlike in the old days.

And here's where the endless queues for Upton Park tube station used to stand, marshalled by police on horses. This was our field of dreams back in the 1970s and early 1980s, when West Ham used to win trophies. There were no World Cups in Qatar then.

It feels like it's going to be a long season. But at least we can sit back in front of the TV for a winter World Cup and hope for better to come from the Hammers after the break.

5

KICKED UP THE ARSENAL

DECEMBER 2022

The World Cup in Qatar provides plenty of West Ham interest. Rice has a solid tournament for England. He is excellent in the quarter-final against France, until it all goes a bit Spursy for Harry Kane who uncharacteristically misses a penalty in the 2–1 defeat. Aguerd impresses as Morocco keep several clean sheets, before he succumbs to injury and misses the semi-final. Paquetá looks a much better player for Brazil in a slightly deeper role, and his goal against South Korea is celebrated with some fine synchronised dancing.

There's even a West Ham connection among the eventual winners, Lionel Messi's Argentina. Manager Lionel Scaloni is a former West Ham loanee. Though I'm sure he would exchange his World Cup medal to be able to go back in time to the 2006 FA Cup final and boot the ball into touch rather than gift Liverpool possession, allowing Steven Gerrard to score from thirty-five yards out.

France include West Ham's second-choice goalkeeper Areola on the bench in the final. Hammers hero Geoff Hurst loses his claim to be the only player to score a hat-trick in a World Cup final when France's Kylian Mbappé scores three times in the 3–3 draw and 4–2 penalty loss to Argentina. Though, as Matt comments, Hurst didn't need penalties to score a hat-trick and ended up on the winning side. And all his goals were definitely over the line.

Meanwhile, some friendlies have been going on at home to keep the players match fit. Matt has taken Lisa on a romantic date to Fulham versus West Ham at a freezing and near-empty Craven Cottage. He reports that getting in proved positively Kafkaesque, thanks to hardly any turnstiles being open. His mood isn't improved when, ten minutes in, Scamacca is hurt following a late tackle from former Hammer Issa Diop and has to leave the field with a serious-looking injury. The friendly ends in a 1–1 draw, and Matt shares some pictures of a snowy Bishop's Palace near the ground, claiming you didn't get that on Green Street. Though Michael points out that Ken's Cafe was a palace of fine cuisine.

The second half of the season begins with a Boxing Day game at Arsenal. We've spent Christmas Day at Nicola's brother's house near Bishop's Stortford before returning to London.

My daughter Lola's boyfriend Michael, a Gooner, has got me a ticket for the match as a Christmas present. His mate has forgotten the password for his online account and there's a nervy wait while Michael has to go to the box office to buy a paper ticket, but eventually, he succeeds. Nigel and Matt also have tickets acquired from Arsenal fans.

Undercover agents Nigel, Matt and I rendezvous at my safe north London house, ready to infiltrate the home fans. Matt has a bad back and looks as mobile as Iain Dowie but spectates through the pain barrier. As we leave my gate, a rather beery Gooner comes up to us.

'Are you lads Arsenal fans?' asks the Gooner. It is then that Nigel denies his religion and mumbles assent. 'Course you are, you couldn't be anything else living round here!'

We then learn that our new friend, who might have been at the Christmas sauce, only got a keyring for Christmas from his missus while all their money went on his kids. It's not easy being a double agent.

At the ground, we separate into our seats borrowed from absent Arsenal fans. As I take my seat behind the goal, I notice that two seats away from me is my near-neighbour Lee, another undercover Hammer marooned in Finsbury Park. We exchange meaningful glances. My daughter Lola is also among the Arsenal fans next to the Hammers contingent.

The game begins with an Arsenal flag being passed over my head and chants of 'Stick your f***ing bubbles up your arse!' The home fans are thinking they are going to win the league. Bukayo Saka has an early goal disallowed for being offside, and the Arsenal players move the ball around crisply. But Bowen and Antonio are causing some problems for the Arsenal defence. When Bowen has his leg taken away by William Saliba, the Irons win a penalty. Despite the Gooners fans waving their arms in the air to distract him, Benrahma sticks it down the middle and scores. I do my best to look depressed.

Coufal and Bowen pick up bookings, but the team are working hard, and Rice is looking strong in midfield. It's tough defending though and Arsenal are awarded a penalty in added time. Thanks to VAR, it's correctly overturned as the ball has struck Cresswell's head, not his hand. The Arsenal fans howl with rage. Incredibly, we're ahead at the break.

At half-time I meet Agent Nigel for a chat and then in the gents spot an Arsenal fan carrying a D. H. Lawrence *The Lost Girl* Penguin Classics tote bag, which seems very Highbury. Matt reveals on WhatsApp that at the bar the Tempranillo Shiraz is temporarily unavailable and the Flowerhead Merlot will be served instead, which is possibly peak middle-class Arsenal.

The second half begins with Antonio getting through but having his shot smothered by Aaron Ramsdale. Arsenal step up a gear and their intricate passing patterns cause big problems – they also start to put themselves about a lot more. The equaliser comes when Martin Ødegaard's shot is deflected into the path of Saka, who has been played onside by Coufal. He slots it home without fuss. Sod it.

The home fans start to ecstatically chant 'There's only one Arsène Wenger!' as their legendary former manager is spotted in the stand. The second goal arrives five minutes after the equaliser. The pacy Gabriel Martinelli looks likely to cross but catches Fabiański out at his near post. 'We are top of the league!' chant the home fans.

The third goal arrives as Eddie Nketiah rolls Kehrer too easily and slots home a good finish. I'm hugged by the ecstatic Gunners fan next to me. That's all I need. 'Are you Tottenham in disguise?' asks the North Bank.

Arsenal look like they could win the league on this form but West Ham do keep going. It's good to see young Mubama get eight minutes at the end and sub Fornals forces Ramsdale to make an excellent late save. We never expected to get too much out of this, and at least we have given them a game, though the side has conceded three poor goals. That's four league defeats in a row now.

Agents Matt and Nigel meet back at my house to discuss D. H. Lawrence and Wainwright wall charts over tea and Proper Job. Football is back. Arsenal will turn over a lot of teams, but now our old/new home season starts with the visit of the bus stop in Hounslow, aka Brentford. The new signings have to gel into a team and quickly.

Four days later, West Ham end the year with a Friday night home fixture against Brentford. Possibly confused by the merging of days in the festive season, Nigel has arrived at the Best Cafe on Thursday night, wondering why there's no one in West Ham shirts and nothing about the game in the paper. After realising his mistake, he foolishly elects to come again the next night and join Matt, Lisa, Fraser, Michael and myself at the London Stadium. I'm wearing my 'I'm Forever Blowing Baubles' West Ham Christmas jumper, which was a present from Nicola – though Matt thinks I might be having myself in dodgy gear.

Nigel might not know what day it is, but he is excited by the pre-match entertainment, including 'The Trooper' by Iron Maiden as well as applause for Pelé, who died earlier in the week.

The West Ham side looks good on paper, with Souček, Kehrer and Antonio dropped, Ogbonna in at centre-back, Paquetá playing deeper and Scamacca back up front. The Hammers start well, with some crisp passing and Rice firing a great effort against the outside of the post. For the first twenty minutes the Irons dominate, with Dawson heading narrowly wide from a corner and Bowen having a close-range shot blocked. Dawson also has a strong appeal for a penalty ignored.

But goals change games, and Brentford score from a simple flick-on after a long throw. Nørgaard's shot is well-saved by

Fabiański, but Ivan Toney is quicker to react than Cresswell or Emerson and pokes home the rebound. We could do without his crossed-hammers celebration.

West Ham respond with further pressure, with Rice and Benrahma prominent and good work by Ogbonna setting Emerson up for a shot that is parried by David Raya. But the second goal is a killer, coming just before the interval. Another throw-on is flicked on and Cresswell is embarrassingly out-paced and out-muscled by Josh Dasilva, who fires into the corner with a good finish. Cresswell has been a great player for West Ham over the years but is clearly losing his pace.

The Hammers almost get back into it at the start of the second half as the ref awards a penalty for Ben Mee's foul on Bowen. Except VAR rules the foul was outside the box, and the free kick comes to nothing. West Ham toil away without looking like scoring. Paquetá, so good for Brazil in the World Cup, misplaces simple passes and the £30 million Scamacca looks lethargic, though he does come to life to test Raya with a stinging shot he can't hold. Moyes plays Scamacca and Antonio together for half an hour, though neither striker looks like they can read the other's play.

Dawson gets in a header from a corner that Raya does well to tip over, but Brentford see out the game fairly comfortably, and Fabiański has to produce a great low save to prevent it being 3–0. 'Show some urgency; just get it in the f**king box!'

shouts a possible vicar's daughter behind us. Antonio sums it up by bustling past three players only to take a comical air kick and miss the ball.

Even Fraser is beginning to lose faith in Moyes. We could probably make Pelé look poor on this form. 'Saïd Benrahma, he wants to come home!' chant the jubilant Brentford fans at their former star.

So, it's five defeats in a row and Moyes is now under serious pressure, despite the good work of the last two and a half seasons. Should West Ham lose any or all of the next three games against Leeds, Wolves and Everton he will surely be out, though there aren't too many options to replace him. After the game, the boss says that we aren't getting much luck and played well in the first half. But it used to be West Ham who were clinical on the break, and we are giving away silly goals. Brentford have joined Brighton as West Ham's unlikely bogey team.

We exit for the Refreshment Room where Michael is taken ill with a dose of ennui and Matt is wondering how he has been overlooked in the New Year Honours List for services to football trivia. Nigel points out, not entirely helpfully, that West Ham have lost nineteen games in 2022.

We've certainly lost a must-win game today with another at Leeds coming up, and once again, we are coming down with the Christmas decorations. The stats show that the Irons had 63 per cent of possession, twenty shots to Brentford's nine and eight corners to Brentford's one. It was a game West Ham should have won but lost through basic defensive errors and lack of creativity in the final third.

A dodgy penalty, a lucky rebound, we desperately need something to turn our season. Who would be a West Ham fan? On my blog, reader MJ sums up the day well with the comment, 'Bielsa keeps getting a mention… pouring down, rubbish performance and signal failure on the way home… Happy New Year all!'

6

EL SACKICO

JANUARY 2023

The new year begins with West Ham and Moyes in deep trouble, having lost five games in a row. The team is trying to transition from a counter-attacking side to a possession outfit, but the suspicion remains that the club has bought too many Rolls-Royce players who don't fancy a relegation fight.

It's been a strange year for West Ham. The highlight of 2022 was undoubtedly the great run to the semi-final of the Europa League. The memories still linger of victory over Sevilla. The London Stadium finally started to feel like home as goals from Souček and Ukrainian Yarmolenko, so soon after the Russian invasion of his country, earned a superb win on an emotional night. The side also surpassed all expectations when, after drawing at home, they won 3–0 at Lyon, who had a gifted midfielder called Lucas Paquetá in their ranks.

But in the league, the side had faltered alongside the Europa run and were grinding out results at home and often underperforming away, without offering much in the way of free-flowing football. Then there was catgate, a bizarre incident even by West Ham standards, when Zouma was fined by the club for kicking his family cat after his brother posted some rather unwise footage of the incident online. For a time, he seemed tabloid enemy number one, though the Ukraine war soon put this in perspective. Zouma was later given a twelve-month community order and was fined and banned from keeping cats for five years after pleading guilty to two charges under the Animal Welfare Act at Thames Magistrates' Court.

Seventh was a decent placing at the end of 2021–22, but it looked like it would end up being better for a long time. While this season, the team have a great record in the Europa Conference but are now in a relegation scrap with a squad of tired-looking players and misfiring new signings. The talent is there, but the players need to realise the seriousness of the situation. The Wednesday night fixture at Leeds United looks ominous.

In *The Guardian*, Jacob Steinberg suggests that Moyes has clashed with some senior players and wonders if sticking with Moyes is too risky:

> Something has to change. Moyes keeps saying that West Ham

just need a break. He spoke positively on Tuesday and does not deserve an undignified exit after all he has done for the club. A defiant showing against Leeds could shift the narrative. But the board must be realistic if there is no sign of any change. The evidence is piling up and West Ham cannot afford to wait too long.

Just to compound West Ham's sense of crisis, on the day of the Leeds match the news comes through that co-chairman David Gold has died at the age of eighty-six. Gold, David Sullivan and Karren Brady have remained unpopular with many fans. Though when I interviewed Gold at his house some years ago, he seemed to be a genuine fan of West Ham with pictures of the play-off final on the wall. He was eager to describe visiting Upton Park as a boy and clearly had a great sense of pride at growing up in poverty at 442 Green Street but ending up co-owning West Ham. And for all the criticism, the co-owners have certainly backed Moyes with nearly £170 million of signings this season. You'd hope the side might put in a performance for Gold at Elland Road.

It's a nerve-shredding evening listening to the radio commentary from Elland Road. On WhatsApp, we learn that Michael is listening with Harry the – possibly lucky – cat and that Matt, Lisa and Nigel are discussing commemorative Iron Maiden stamps. At least we have competitive groundhopping, with Nigel having seen Enfield Town beat Haringey

Borough 2–1 and Matt at the Skyline Roofing Stadium aka Northwood Park aka Chestnut Avenue to watch Northwood FC lose 4–1 at home to Hanworth Villa.

After a respectful tribute to Gold, the Hammers make a lively start but are again undone by a throw-in, as Crysencio Summerville sets up Wilfried Gnonto to score with a crisp finish. Kehrer is looking out of position at left-back (why not play Emerson there if Cresswell is dropped?) and we fear the worst. But the Hammers keep going and Coufal almost catches out Illan Meslier with a long-distance lob.

With half-time approaching, Scamacca feeds the ball inside and Bowen is brought down in the box. The ref plays a good advantage only for Fornals to shoot wide of an open goal. Luckily, VAR intervenes, and the penalty is given. Paquetá does a stop-start run-up and expertly puts it in the top corner with a classy penalty for his first West Ham goal. It would have looked terrible if he'd missed but that confidence is surely the sign of a quality player.

A minute into the second half, West Ham are ahead. Brenden Aaronson plays a loose ball to Scamacca, who fires home a great low strike from twenty-five yards out that goes in off the post. As Moyes says, a little cuttingly, Scamacca should be getting tap-ins too, but that strike is evidence that he can be a bit special.

It's a good chance to get three points, but when Jack Harrison comes on, Leeds put the Irons under heavy pressure.

Rice is caught trying to mark two players and Rodrigo fires home another quality finish.

Willed on by a passionate crowd, Leeds go for the winner. Fabiański has to tip over from Rodrigo and Antonio clears a header off the line. For the Irons, sub Benrahma causes problems on the break and his cross is very nearly put into the net by fellow sub Antonio. It's left to Fabiański to gain a point with the last action of five added minutes as he claws away Rodrigo's header with a brilliant reaction save.

It's been a great game for the neutral and in the end, the Hammers are grateful for a point that ends the run of five successive defeats – though it was also a missed opportunity. Defeat would have seen us slip into the bottom three, so an away point is still some kind of progress.

Saturday does see a much-needed win, though it's in the FA Cup, which is almost an afterthought in view of the troubled league form. Still, Moyes takes it seriously. Apart from Coufal, who was crocked by a bad Summerville foul at Leeds, and Scamacca, who is feeling his knee, Moyes plays a full-strength side. Brentford play a side of mostly squad players.

It's a poor game. Yoane Wissa and Keane Lewis-Potter have a couple of half-chances for Brentford, and Souček misses a really good chance after being set up by Emerson. It isn't settled until the seventy-ninth minute when Rice makes a great tackle to free sub Benrahma, who shoots from distance and scores. It's a good swerving strike, though Brentford reserve keeper Thomas Strakosha should have done better. Benrahma, who refuses to celebrate against his former side, now has six goals and is West Ham's second-top scorer.

'I think the result in midweek and a good win here today is something to build on,' says Moyes. 'Getting through in any cup competition is important and we just about got there today. I said last week we could do with someone scoring a screamer and Saïd did that. His impact was excellent. It was a terrific goal.'

It is a good psychological boost to win any game and particularly against Brentford, who have defeated the Irons in all three games since promotion. So, the mooted cup final breakfast at Nigel's gaff in Kew remains on – just.

Another difficult away game follows at Wolves. Moyes opts for safety first, as ever, and drops Benrahma. The out-of-form Antonio is favoured over Scamacca. Dawson is also left out with a move to Wolves a possibility, though it would be sad to lose him.

Wolves have the better of a dull first half, but the Irons do have the best chance when, after a tussle with Bowen, the ball falls to Coufal who scuffs his shot into a Wolves defender. 'Another of those games where we're not really doing enough,' comments Fraser on WhatsApp.

'At least you didn't go to Stevenage to watch the Under-21s only for it to be postponed because of a waterlogged pitch, leaving you in Stevenage,' replies Matt.

'Always good to know you're not in Stevenage,' agrees Fraser.

After a decent start to the second half from the Irons, the winner comes from a West Ham corner. Wolves clear from their six-yard box and break at speed. The ball deflects rather unluckily off Cresswell and into the path of Podence, who lashes it home with a fine finish from the edge of the box. 'Wolves score few and concede relatively few; we're in trouble now,' comments Matt from the wilds of Stevenage.

The Hammers improve after Benrahma and Scamacca come on, but Moyes's side can't keep waiting until the final twenty minutes to start playing. Wolves are unlucky when Neves hits the bar and then Rayan Aït-Nouri strikes the rebound against the post. Benrahma does force Sá into a save and late on Scamacca heads wide, but it never seems that likely the Hammers will equalise. West Ham are in the bottom three.

'That's one point in seven games for Moyes and one win in the last ten. Surely that's sackable. There must be people on the phone to Sullivan all the time offering alternatives,' says Fraser on WhatsApp. 'When we played Wolves last season, we were third. Now we're third from bottom,' is the damning fact that Nigel produces.

All confidence seems to have gone from the likes of Bowen, Antonio, Souček and Scamacca, while the £50 million Paquetá is still underperforming. The only positive is that Zouma returned from injury to make the bench at Wolves. It seems very unlikely that both Moyes and Frank Lampard can survive next week's relegation six-pointer with Everton. League form has been poor for a year now, and as the Stranglers once sang, 'Something Better Change'.

The papers have their say on the clash now billed as El Sackico. In *The Times*, Martin Samuel writes a column headlined, 'West Ham's conundrum: the ideal replacement for David Moyes is… David Moyes.' He explains:

> Here is the conundrum. Lose at home to Everton on Saturday and it is possible it will be decided that David Moyes is no longer the man for the job. The type of manager the club would require, however, is a pragmatic organiser capable of steering them away from relegation. If he was available, West Ham would go for David Moyes.

Is it time to panic? It's worth noting that most of those online critics who now call him an outdated dinosaur were also praising him last season. But the bad run is still massively worrying. A loss to Everton would mean one point from eight games. This season, it seems that other teams have rumbled Moyes's system of a deep defensive block with West Ham scoring on the break or from set-pieces, while the expensive new signings are floundering.

Ideally, West Ham will beat Everton and retain Moyes.

Having allowed him to spend close to £170 million last summer, it makes sense to allow him time to change tactics, get his new signings firing and avoid the upheaval of a new manager wanting to change the squad yet again. There is half a season left, and if the side's luck can turn, Moyes would surely have enough know-how to keep the side up.

Should the team lose to Everton and fire Moyes then what are the options? Mauricio Pochettino and Thomas Tuchel are out of West Ham's league. Sean Dyche has the most impressive record of the unemployed gaffers and can certainly motivate players, though would the crowd take to his route one style, and can he deal with star players? Rafael Benítez would be very defensive, and Wolves's former boss Nuno Espírito Santo did well in the Midlands but was very reliant on an influx of Portuguese talent and failed at Spurs. And there's always the chance Sullivan would go for Big Sam again. West Ham's best hope might be if Chelsea lost patience with Graham Potter. Stick or twist, it's not going to be easy.

But while El Sackico looms, the transfer window is open and two significant events happen. Dawson departs to Wolves for £3.3 million as he wants to be closer to the Midlands for family reasons. The Rochdale Beckenbauer has gained something of a cult following during his three seasons at West Ham. Dawson might not be the most skilful player in the world but he relishes the ugly part of defending and has to be one of the best at blocks in the Premier League. He always showed massive commitment, which West Ham fans love.

Dawson was very underrated and was a better signing than James Tarkowski, for whom West Ham once bid £30 million. He was also extremely useful at set-pieces and scored a lot of goals for a centre-back, including the opener in the memorable 3–0 win at Lyon last season. And there was a nerveless penalty against Man City in a victorious Carabao Cup shoot-out. Dawson is pushing thirty-three, and the Hammers now have a lot of centre-backs, having signed Aguerd and Kehrer. But you certainly wouldn't want to be on the wrong end of one of his tackles. Thank you for the daze, Craig.

In a more telling development, Moyes makes an unexpected signing, with Danny Ings arriving from Aston Villa for a reported £15 million. Ings could be just what West Ham need. He's not a particularly sexy signing but the thirty-year-old is a proven goal scorer. He's scored every three games throughout his career and averaged close to one every two games for Burnley. A move to Liverpool was ruined by an ACL injury and then a bad knee injury to his other leg. But with the aid of careful rehabilitation and Pilates he flourished at Southampton, scoring forty-one goals in ninety-one games.

Seventeen months ago, Aston Villa paid £30 million for Ings. Despite being deemed expendable by Unai Emery, he has bagged six goals for Villa so far this season. Ings has scored more than a hundred goals in his career, and with

Antonio ageing and Scamacca struggling, his poaching could be vital. He's also the source of a good stat, which Matt promptly points out on WhatsApp. Ings will now have played for all three clubs to play in the Premier League in claret and blue – Burnley, Villa and West Ham.

The morning of the Everton game arrives. The Toffees are struggling too, and boss Frank Lampard, our ex-player, could well go if they lose the game. *The Times* features the worrying statistic that West Ham have won eight games in Europe and only four in the league. In a perverse kind of way, I've missed relegation struggles. Looking down instead of up, checking the fixtures of the other teams likely to go down. Moyes said he planned to end West Ham's reputation as being 'flaky' when he arrived. Now we're back to being flakier than a Cadbury Flake 99 and reprising the bad old days of really pepping it up and making it mediocre. Two seasons in the top seven was a mirage. This is what West Ham do. Twenty-five more points and we're safe.

It's off to the Best Meze cafe for pre-match fine cuisine, where Nigel says he has ticked off a new ground at Haringey Borough FC. The bad news is that he has forgotten his lucky banana.

We're joined by Michael, Matt and Lisa. Our party is left reeling by some inflationary price increases, as my egg, chips and beans and a cup of tea now costs £8, and Michael needs a second mortgage to buy his omelette and chips. Maybe new

Chancellor Jeremy Hunt could explain it all in a video with some coffee cups.

We meet Fraser in the ground, where Mark Noble is on the pitch with the family of David Gold in a tribute to West Ham's late chairman. Moyes has dropped Souček in order to play Paquetá alongside Rice in central midfield. Emerson is in for Cresswell and the returning Zouma partners Aguerd and Ogbonna in central defence, in what looks like our best available side.

There's an early fashion faux pas in the Billy Bonds Stand as we spot that Matt's yellow hoodie matches Everton's away strip. It's an understandably nervous start from both sides, with two sets of five-man defences, an early Everton claim for handball in the box and an injury scare to Zouma, who plays on rather like Monty Python's Black Knight.

The nerves of the home fans are improved when Benrahma finally gets a shot away towards the top corner, which Jordan Pickford tips over. The crucial goal arrives after thirty-four minutes. A West Ham corner is cleared but wing-back Emerson pings in another cross. Zouma gets a head to it and in nips Bowen to score. There's a nervy VAR pause, but Jarrod proves to be onside by the width of Tarkowski's boot. He celebrates the news that he is having twins with Dani Dyer by stuffing the ball up his shirt and sucking both thumbs. It's Bowen's first goal in ten games and just the confidence boost he needs.

Five minutes later, the second goal arrives. Antonio is too quick for a rash tackle by Tarkowski and escapes down the right flank. His cross is swept home by Bowen who has managed to get ahead of two defenders. Never in doubt!

There's a scare before half-time as Alex Iwobi's shot is deflected by Rice against the outside of the post, but the Irons go in at the break two goals ahead. In the concourse, we meet Steve the industrial action-taking Cornish postie, who has travelled up from the West Country in the belief that West Ham need all the strikers they can get. Though he still doesn't know where my Christmas cards are.

The second half sees Everton have a lot of possession as Dominic Calvert-Lewin almost gets on the end of an Iwobi cross. But Zouma is solid and Aguerd has a fine game at the back. The best two chances fall to West Ham on the break. A brilliant return ball from Benrahma sets Emerson free, and the left-back's shot is tipped on to the bar by Pickford. When Benrahma cleverly finds Rice on the halfway line, Rice surges into the Toffees' box to fire across goal and just wide.

Ings gets to come on for Antonio and then Moyes goes slightly sub crazy, bringing on Johnson, Souček and Downes. The home fans get to sing their 'Big Fat Frankie Lampard!' song and a chorus of 'You're getting sacked in the morning!' The away fans are dispirited, and it's hard not to feel sorry for the Everton supporters. The club has burned through a lot of managers who have done better elsewhere, like Marco Silva, and wasted a lot of money on sub-standard players. A lack of goals in the side is their big problem, while Lampard has inherited a squad put together by six different gaffers.

Aguerd, Rice, Benrahma and Bowen have all had big games. At the final whistle, Oggy does a celebration jig for the fans. This is a much-needed win for West Ham and with the squad we have, surely the side can reach mid-table. Finally, Moyes has been able to field Zouma and Aguerd together and the defence has looked much more solid. The arrival of Ings means the Hammers have an unprecedented three strikers at the club.

Matt and Lisa depart to see The Delgados at Shepherd's Bush, while the rest of us head off to The Eagle, unfamiliar with the sensation of celebrating a West Ham win. There's Doom Bar in the fridge and 'Zombie' on the jukebox. Fraser, who never doubted the Moyesiah (much), has now struck up a friendship with Sinead at the bar, resulting in table service for our party. Nigel wonders if there is a Deep Purple musical he can visit with his birthday vouchers. With games against Newcastle, Chelsea and Spurs coming up, we can't be complacent. But this is more like it from the Irons.

Moyes has remained admirably calm throughout a high-pressure week. He tells Gary Lineker on *Match of the Day*:

I've been pretty cool about it, if that's the right word. I've had

> great support from the board and behind the scenes knowing they're so keen for me to stay and do well. We've changed a lot of players, a decision we took last March when we weren't quite getting the results in the run-in. The change has been difficult but I think the new players we've brought in can become really good players here.

Lampard is duly sacked by Everton, though the win also proves costly for West Ham. Ings seemed fine giving interviews after the match but now we learn he has a 'slight knee injury' after a late tackle that will keep him out for a few games. With Scamacca also struck by a troublesome injury that leaves West Ham back with Antonio as the only fit striker. At least Antonio had a decent game against Everton. But after Aguerd's injury in his first friendly at Rangers, you do wonder if there is an unwritten rule that any new signing must get injured in their first match and that Antonio must always be our only striker.

Then, reports claim that Zouma could be out for up to a month with the thigh injury he picked up during the first half. We could see from the Billy Bonds Stand that he was struggling, and it was a surprise that he played on through some obvious discomfort. Zouma really should have been subbed – historically West Ham seem to have a problem with not taking off injured players. We recall Andy Carroll once making a bad injury worse by playing on at Southampton.

It was a must-win game, but with Ogbonna and Aguerd on the pitch, caution would have been advisable. This has happened just when Moyes was finally getting his best two centre-backs, Zouma and Aguerd, forming an effective partnership. The only positives are that there's a two-week gap until the next league game at Newcastle and Zouma is a quick healer.

The month ends with an FA Cup tie at Derby County, screened live on a Monday evening. Though it's nice of the FA to ruin it for us by having the draw just before kick-off – and yet again, West Ham are drawn away to Man United. That's three times we've drawn the Mancs away in cup competitions in the last three seasons.

Derby are now a League One club, with a fine stadium but not much brass, but at least they are still in existence, which was in doubt last year. The Irons start well, with Downes making a fine tackle to release Bowen who fires at the keeper. After ten minutes comes a welcome opener to deflate the crowd. Antonio's shot is blocked, but Downes plays a short ball to Souček who plays a one-two with Antonio. Souček unselfishly heads Antonio's return across the goal for Bowen to fire home.

Derby rarely threaten and the ITV4 viewers get plenty of time to admire Aguerd's control and left foot passes. Antonio and Bowen are lively up front and Fornals dithers when he should shoot. 'How shit must you be / We're winning away!'

chant the West Ham fans, followed by 'My name is Luděk Miklośko...'

The second half sees the game put to bed as Fornals pounces on some lax midfield play to put in a through ball that is deflected to Bowen. Bowen's cross nicks a defender and sits up nicely for Antonio to head home.

The rest of the game is spent enjoying the away fans' rather impolite songs about Frank Lampard. Bowen should make it three after sub Benrahma plays him through, and young Mubama comes on and does a few bits of good hold-up play.

So, a fairly easy win without the rested Rice and Paquetá and now a massive task at Old Trafford in the next round of the FA Cup. I do fear our cup final breakfast in Kew might just be postponed for another season. But more importantly, Premier League survival needs to be secured.

7

THERE'S NOBODY BETTER THAN LUCAS PAQUETÁ

FEBRUARY 2023

Newcastle away is the sort of difficult away match West Ham have been losing all season. Buoyed by Saudi Arabian cash and the astute signings of Eddie Howe, the Magpies are making a solid bid for the top four.

When Newcastle score after forty seconds, it looks like being a long afternoon. Joe Willock's effort is correctly disallowed by VAR as the ball has gone out of play, but from the resulting goal kick, Newcastle score a legitimate goal. Paquetá isn't strong enough in midfield, Sean Longstaff nicks the ball and plays a through pass to Callum Wilson, who always scores against us. Wilson has managed to get between Ogbonna and Kehrer for a simple finish. It's a poor goal to concede.

Fabian Schär then flicks a free kick over the bar, but the response from West Ham is good. The players look angry, and driven on by the excellent Rice, the Irons start to have the better of the half. Emerson makes a number of surging runs and after good work by Antonio, Benrahma shoots on his right foot instead of taking it on his left.

When Paquetá has an effort deflected narrowly wide, the Irons win a corner. I'm wondering why Rice is taking it when he would surely be more use in the box. He answers my doubts by whipping in an excellent inswinger, which is flicked on by Aguerd. Paquetá is on hand at the far post to control and calmly poke over the line. He celebrates his second goal for the Irons with an audacious double somersault, something not even Antonio has attempted after scoring. Benrahma cuts inside, only to fire wide from a good position and then Aguerd puts a free header over the bar from Coufal's free kick. So, it's 1–1 at the break.

The Hammers start the second half well, with Johnson on for the injured Kehrer. But the last half an hour sees considerable Newcastle pressure. Coufal blocks Allan Saint-Maximin's goal-bound effort, Joelinton is booked for a terrible dive and Newcastle's best chance is a Callum Wilson header straight at Fabiański.

Aguerd has a great game at the back and his best moment is a sprint back to make a superb tackle on Wilson just as the forward is about to shoot. Credit to Coufal too for another well-timed tackle on Saint-Maximin in the box.

In the end, it's a very creditable away point and one of the best performances of the season. Newcastle looked a little tired after reaching the League Cup final in midweek and they missed Bruno Guimarães. But, even so, this was a solid team performance from West Ham. Even my fellow season ticket holder Matt is impressed and for the first time in his life says on WhatsApp that he 'thought the ref had a good game'.

This was more like last season and gives the side something to build on. A couple of days after the Newcastle game, Leeds United sack Jesse Marsch, leaving West Ham as the only team in the bottom six not to sack their manager. On the evidence of the game at St James' Park, the board might be right to hold their nerve.

Next up is Chelsea, who have signed seventeen players and spent a total of around £550 million this season. *The Guardian* reports that Chelsea's gross transfer expenditure in the January transfer window 'was more than the combined total of all clubs in the Bundesliga, La Liga, Serie A and Ligue 1'. Owner Todd Boehly's bizarre strategy is to use creative accounting to spread the cost of the deals over eight-year contracts (next season they'll only be allowed to spread costs over five years) and keep within the financial fair play rules.

It's a risky game as you can end up with a lot of dud players on long-term contracts. Imagine if West Ham had signed Anderson, Haller, Jordan Hugill, Roberto, Ajeti and Wilshere on eight-year deals. It's surprising to see Chelsea's new gaffer Graham Potter mixed up in all this, as at Brighton he was known for sensible management. His biggest problem will be keeping a massive squad happy. They might need to hire the whole of the Westfield shopping centre as their dressing room. The good news is that only sixteen of them can play against the Irons.

We're in the Best Cafe at the slightly unreal time of 11.30 a.m. for a 12.30 p.m. kick-off against the Blues. The omelettes are off so Lisa and I opt for mushrooms on toast, and Michael braves a full breakfast. Nigel is looking forward to seeing Girlschool later (though surely they must be sixth-formers by now?) and Matt manages to namedrop that he's read some good trivia about Jock Stein in the Northwood versus Hanworth Villa programme. Lisa and Matt have already seen West Ham's women's side lose 7–0 to Chelsea this week and hope a similar score isn't about to happen again today.

It's on to the London Stadium where there are big queues at the security points. There's almost a sold-out programme disaster before Nigel and myself find one at the tent just past the security checks. We miss the first four minutes but get in just in time to see Paquetá get fouled, fall over and then go off with a shoulder injury. Souček replaces him. Chelsea are fielding a £200 million forward line in a side of mainly young players selected from their massive squad.

Early on, João Félix gets behind West Ham's defence to hit the post and tap home the rebound. It's disallowed for offside, correctly, but it's a warning. West Ham have the relatively new centre-back partnership of Ogbonna and Aguerd and look tentative at the back. The Hammers start slowly, and when £107 million signing Enzo Fernández has time to chip a through ball to Félix, who has got behind Aguerd too easily, it's 1–0 legitimately. Bowen might have been fouled in the build-up but it's still a sloppy goal to concede. Kai Havertz thinks he's made it 2–0, only to be ruled offside again.

After a poor opening twenty minutes, the Hammers come to life and start pressing Kepa and his defenders as they try to play it out of defence. Bowen gets a low cross in from the left and Antonio flicks it against Kepa's body to raise the hopes of the home crowd.

The equaliser arrives on twenty-eight minutes. Kehrer finds Coufal in space on the right, and the wing-back's cross is flicked on by Bowen. Antonio can't reach it, but Emerson is at the back post and the old prog rocker scuffs it home. Emerson refuses to celebrate against his former club but everyone else does.

Before the break, Fabiański has to produce a good save to deny the £30 million Noni Madueke, and it's level at half-time. The second half sees a resilient performance from the

Irons. Rice shoots narrowly wide, while Antonio heads a Chelsea free kick just wide of his own net. The traditional folk song of 'From Stamford Bridge to Upton Park / Stick your blue flag up your arse' reverberates around the London Stadium.

Just as Nigel wonders if Chelsea's Marc Cucurella could be in Metallica, the hirsute and out-of-form left-back is replaced by Chilwell, who whinges at the ref and lino for much of his cameo. Souček is having a decent workmanlike game after coming on as an early sub and it could go either way. It seems like he might have won it for the Irons after eighty-one minutes. Sub Ings wins a free kick, taken by Emerson. Rice's header is saved by Kepa and Souček taps home the rebound. But VAR intervenes and deems that Rice's shoulder is marginally offside. It's always annoying to leap out of your seat for nothing thanks to Stockley Park.

Worryingly, Aguerd goes off with a knock, so we have to hope he and Paquetá are not too badly hurt. At least Kehrer has a decent second half. There's still time for more controversy. Conor Gallagher's shot is blocked by a falling Souček and hits the non-bouncing Czech's hand. It should be a penalty, but after Cornetgate at Stamford Bridge we deserve some luck with VAR. Graham Potter describes it as a 'great save'.

So, the Hammers are unbeaten in four matches and have drawn against Newcastle and Chelsea, games we were expected to lose. We head to The Eagle where Sinead has laid on bottles of Whitstable Bay organic ale for me and cheese sandwiches for Fraser, as we wonder whatever happened to the injured and unseen Cornet. The pub is packed for the rugby, but we sit in the beer garden waiting for Matt and Lisa to arrive from the club shop, probably laden with West Ham dog bowls and the last few Arthur Masuaku mugs.

Chelsea should always beat us, having spent so much on players (are they part of Liz Truss's 'left-wing economic establishment'?). So, a point is a decent result thanks to Souček's save of the day.

However, the injury to Paquetá keeps the Brazilian playmaker out of the game at Spurs and allows Moyes to give in to his at times over-cautious nature. It's a strange defensive line-up, with the limited Downes in midfield alongside Rice and Souček. Surely Fornals or Benrahma would have offered more going forward? Playing for a goalless draw is far too unambitious against a Spurs side that has lost its goalkeeper Lloris and has a caretaker manager in Cristian Stellini after the implosion of Antonio Conte, who basically ranted that the players and board were rubbish.

Agent Nigel has infiltrated the home fans with his lucky banana. The Irons start well, with Souček playing in Bowen for a volley that flies wide in the first minute. West Ham force a few corners but still look unthreatening from set-pieces, while Spurs have a penalty appeal waved away after the falling

Kehrer touches the ball with his hand. The Hammers frustrate Spurs in a dull first half, and the only real action is a late shot from Richarlison that Fabiański saves with his legs.

After the break, Spurs come out with greater purpose. Mistakes from Aguerd and Rice present chances to Richarlison and Kane. The breakthrough comes when Højbjerg plays a through ball to Ben Davies, which dissects Coufal and Ogbonna too easily. One full-back lays it off to the other, and Emerson Royal calmly slots home. The Hammers have an instant chance to equalise as Antonio's knock-on finds Bowen, who fires against the feet of Fraser Forster.

The game is effectively over when Kane manages to find a little space after a tussle with Ogbonna and plays in substitute Son, who scores with another calm finish after getting beyond Coufal and Kehrer. Moyes waits too long to bring on Benrahma and Ings, and later Fornals and Johnson, and the Irons never really look like getting a goal back. Bowen does well on the right to set up Benrahma who shoots way wide.

To compound the misery, my daughter Nell is there with her Spurs-supporting boyfriend and sends a video of the home fans singing 'West Ham get battered everywhere they go!' as they chuck Beavertown beer over each other.

It's not a terrible performance, but it was, as *The Guardian* put it, 'doggedly mediocre'. Moyes still sees 'a lot of good things' in the performance, though criticises the defending and the lack of goals from Antonio and Bowen. Rice appears to give some coded criticism of the tactics as he says, 'When you play five at the back and three like we set up today, maybe our forwards felt a little bit isolated when we got the ball to them – they didn't really have enough around them, not enough support.'

One friend says that he is considering boycotting the next home match in protest at this unimaginative performance. It's looking bad again. West Ham need to win some away games and we're not going to do that set up to take a point. The Irons need Zouma and Paquetá fit and to give Ings a chance. Social media can trigger a flight-or-fight response and result in massive over-reactions, but the fans' frustration is understandable.

Pressure is never far away in the Premier League, and it is back on Moyes as the side remain in eighteenth place after one win in eleven games. Sky Sports reports that 'Moyes' three-year stint at the helm is on the rocks.' A stats-based analysis reveals that West Ham have yet to score from a cross this season despite having the third highest total of crosses in the Premier League.

According to expected goals, West Ham should have scored thirty goals but have scored only nineteen. Not only that but West Ham were the top Premier League scorers from headers in 2020–21, but have only scored one header this season, the worst total in the division. The *Daily Mail* points out that the Hammers were the second-best team at scoring set-piece goals in 2020–21 but are now ranking eighteenth. Though strangely, the Hammers are the best team at not conceding goals from corners.

Scoring is the issue. Bowen has shown signs of improvement but has had a disappointing season overall. Antonio, while always putting in a shift, has only scored two league goals. *The Times* reports that Moyes could be sacked should West Ham lose at home to Forest. But sacking the manager could result in a Southampton or Leeds situation where there is no obvious replacement for Nathan Jones or Jesse Marsch. Rafa Benítez is reportedly interested in the West Ham job and has a proven track record, though would the crowd take to another defensive gaffer?

Meanwhile, Moyes perhaps needs saving from himself. As a former defender he does like to play it safe. Surely assistants Kevin Nolan and Mark Warburton should be using their influence to persuade him to not play three holding midfielders at once and make earlier substitutions? His teams can attack – back in 2020–21 West Ham looked lethal counter-attacking away from home, breaking at speed through Lingard, Antonio and Bowen. But all that seems like a long time ago.

Downes is a promising young midfielder and can do a job as a ball-winner, deputising for Souček or Rice. But Moyes seems to have a bizarre penchant for starting him in big away matches. Downes has only started in four matches this season and three of those were Man United away, Liverpool away and Tottenham away. His other start was at home to Bournemouth. If you want to give him experience, then why not try some easier games?

When Downes does come in, it's as part of three holding midfielders, which negates the scoring chances of the team as a whole. Downes was a decent tackler and passer at Swansea but has no goals and no assists this season and has never been known as a goal scorer. He prefers to keep possession rather than try a through ball. Against Spurs, Antonio and Bowen were the only out-and-out attackers. Nor has the tactic worked; in all three of these big away matches the team has lost.

Moyes brings in Downes when he wants to keep things tight, but a team that has spent £160 million in the summer should be better than just trying to keep the score down and nick a late goal. Benrahma, Fornals or Lanzini (and Paquetá when fit) have to return to the side to offer some much-needed creativity.

To be positive, there have been signs of improvement in the performances against Everton, Newcastle and Chelsea, and of the final fifteen matches left, only four are against the current top six. But we desperately need goals, otherwise Moyes could be gone and the Hammers plummeting towards relegation.

The crunch game against fellow strugglers Nottingham Forest comes on Saturday. On the way to the match, Nigel has succumbed to some Moyes kidology, bemoaning the fact that the gaffer has said Danny Ings is 'not ready to start a game for three, four, five weeks'. Yet at 2 p.m. the news comes through that Ings is starting and Paquetá is back. Moyes has picked the side most fans wanted, reverting to a flat back four with Benrahma restored on the left and Johnson, rather surprisingly, replacing Emerson who has been playing quite well.

Perhaps anticipating another drubbing, Michael has brought a pharmacy bag of medication with him, while Matt is chastened to discover that his yellow hoodie is the same as Forest's away kit. There's a tribute to the great Bobby Moore, who died thirty years ago this weekend, before the kick-off and surprisingly, the Hammers start with great intent. The Irons force a series of corners that Keylor Navas punches away, with Benrahma and Bowen looking energetic and Paquetá at last starting to dominate midfield.

Paquetá's low cross is deflected against the outside of the post by Felipe. The Hammers' best chance comes when Ings gets a close-range header all wrong from Coufal's cross. 'If even Ings is missing chances, then we're doomed,' muses Matt.

Having dominated the half, there's a scare at the end as Brennan Johnson goes down under pressure from Ben

Johnson. The ref rules, correctly, that Johnson tumbled rather theatrically after only slight contact.

Nigel takes his lucky banana out of its case at half-time and consumes it to try and change our fortunes. The Irons continue to dominate, despite Coufal going off and being replaced by Cresswell. But we know it isn't our day when, after good build-up play from Paquetá and Benrahma, the hard-working Bowen races through to power a shot against the inside of the post. Seconds later, Paquetá chips just over the bar. At least the crowd comes alive after that, the mood having been quiet and resigned for much of the game. 'Come on you Irons!' booms around the stadium as the sky darkens and rain pounds the grass.

There are more problems as Fabiański takes a knock and has to be replaced by Areola. It's surely drifting towards a goalless draw, but on seventy-one minutes, something incredible happens. Ings plays a good ball out wide to Bowen on the right. Bowen dribbles into the box and Ings sweeps home the cross as the Bobby Moore Stand rises in unison. It's a great finish as the ball is slightly behind him. Ings looks offside, but after a VAR check it's a goal as Ings has timed his run perfectly and is just onside. It's all very confusing as we're just not used to seeing well-timed runs at West Ham.

Two minutes later, Paquetá shows great determination to feed Benrahma on the left. Benrahma skips over a tackle and his cross is bundled home by Ings, who is on the ground but has somehow managed to flick the ball in with his heel. A real poacher's goal. Moyes reprises his Manuel Lanzini at Spurs dad dance.

Then Rice plays a give and go with Benrahma and on the edge of the area sends a sumptuous shot into the top corner to spark jubilation all over the London Stadium. As the late former England gaffer Graham Taylor might say, 'What sort of thing is happening here?'

The crowd start to give every pass an 'Olé!' As an extra bonus, we get the chance to boo Forest subs Lingard and André Ayew, both ex-Hammers. Ings is replaced by Antonio and receives a deserved ovation. He's the first predator in the box we've had since Chicharito.

On eighty-four minutes, Cresswell finds sub Fornals who stands the ball up nicely for Antonio to head home with his first touch. Fraser, who has been known to smoke a cigar for every goal West Ham score, starts to worry as he only has eight cigars with him.

Credit too to sub Areola, who produces a brilliant save from Toffolo late on to preserve a clean sheet. Ogbonna has kept Chris Wood quiet, and with Benrahma getting two assists and West Ham finally scoring from crosses, it's been a good day all round.

Outside the ground, a rainbow rises over Stratford as if to mark the miracle of the Hammers scoring four goals in fourteen minutes. Nigel might even think it's Ritchie Blackmore's

Rainbow. We file off to The Eagle with an air of disbelief and over Whitstable Bay ale amuse ourselves by creating fictional tabloid headlines like '"Moyes must stay" says Fraser'.

When did we last score four? Nigel thinks it was away to Norwich last season. There's a long way to go, but this result brings Forest back into the pack and takes West Ham out of the bottom three. If we can keep playing like this then we'll surely rise up the table.

Quite a few fans pick up on the way Paquetá celebrated Ings's second goal against Nottingham Forest, arms outstretched as if he'd scored himself. Paquetá had done really well to flick the ball over a defender, outmuscle a challenge and find Benrahma, whose run and cross set up Ings. Was that the moment Paquetá showed that he had adapted to the physicality of the Premier League? He has had his best game in a West Ham shirt. He was unlucky not to score, but more importantly he dominated the game, being involved in just about everything in midfield. With Rice disciplined in the holding role and Souček more advanced, the central midfield trio all had good games. It's been a long time coming but finally Paquetá is starting to look like the player the club paid £50 million for.

It's left to Nigel to share a nugget from *The Times*. West Ham became the first team in ten years to win a top-flight game by four goals having been level during the final quarter of the match. And Ings is the first player to score twice in seven minutes for two teams in one season, having earlier performed the same feat for Aston Villa against Brentford. Surely Ings can only get better, and West Ham will soon be moving up the league.

8

YOU DON'T KNOW WHAT YOU'RE DOING!

MARCH 2023

March begins with a trip to Old Trafford in the FA Cup. It seems like a good time to be playing a below-full-strength United side, possibly distracted by their Carabao Cup victory against Newcastle at the weekend, their first trophy for several years. Fabiański has a fractured cheekbone and eye socket after getting caught by a knee in the Forest match. The Irons do have one of the best number twos in the league in Areola though.

Marcel Sabitzer tests Areola early on, but West Ham have the better of the first half. A great ball from Benrahma releases Antonio but he never looks like scoring in a one-on-one with de Gea and waits too long before shooting against the keeper. Antonio always looks better when he doesn't have time to think and strikes the ball instinctively. An Emerson cross fizzes across the goal with Fornals standing still, and that moment reveals just why Moyes opted for a player like Ings to gamble and get in the box.

Casemiro comes on for United at half-time as Erik ten Hag gets worried. The Irons take a deserved lead as United appeal that the ball has gone out for a throw. Souček just about keeps the ball in play and finds Emerson. The left-back passes to Benrahma who arrows a great effort into the top corner. The 4,000 away fans go potty and dream of another Di Canio-esque cup win at Old Trafford.

All seems to be going to plan. Fornals hits a low cross across goal with no one there to tap it home, then Antonio does well to beat Lisandro Martínez for speed but, perhaps haunted by his first-half miss, instead of crossing he fires against de Gea's legs. Two fine saves from de Gea but Antonio seems to have lost the art of good decision making when given time in the box. It proves costly.

Rashford is now on and Casemiro has a header disallowed for offside. On seventy-seven minutes, United win a corner after a miskick by Aguerd. Areola comes but fails to clean out his defenders and Aguerd back-heads the ball into his own net.

The game looks to be going into extra time with ninety minutes gone, but Aguerd slices a clearance to Wout

Weghorst, whose shot deflects to Alejandro Garnacho on the edge of the box. Johnson could be a bit tighter, and the blond winger curls a great finish into the far corner. United score an undeserved third in the fifth minute of added time when poor old Aguerd lets the ball slide under his foot and Fred strikes home. It's been a nightmare for Aguerd, who has been at fault for all three United goals.

On ITV, we then get to see Roy Keane patronise West Ham just to make it a bit worse. So, our FA Cup final breakfast at Nigel's gaff in Kew is cancelled for the seventeenth season running. Though the only time said breakfast brought us any luck was when we dined at Nigel's place before the 2005 play-off final in Cardiff. It's not the despair etc. A good performance for seventy-seven minutes but if you don't take your chances against top sides and then give them an own goal, this is the result. It is now the Europa Conference or nothing in the cup competitions.

That dispiriting defeat at Man United is followed by a daunting away trip to Brighton. Up against a team that we've failed to beat in eleven Premier League games – what could possibly go wrong? Since the stadium move it's been nearly impossible to get away tickets as they go to those who have away season tickets and those who already have a lot of priority points, and they get more with every away game they attend. But for once I'm in luck as my old fanzine-writing pal Big Joe, who is now big in the comedy industry, has contacts at the club and has come up with a pair for the away end at the Amex.

Signal failures at Selhurst suggest it's not going to be a good day as I wait at Victoria. Big Joe is waiting for news at Clapham, while my train eventually moves at the same speed as the West Ham defence. Still, at least Joe has hatched a cunning plan to go to Lewes instead of Brighton and take the local train to Falmer.

In Lewes, we have a decent lunch in a chic cafe, which proves to be the best part of the day, before boarding the train to Falmer, which is again delayed. Somehow, we make it into the away end just in time for kick-off. Brighton's new ground is a long way out of town and is surrounded by green downs. The home crowd is full of optimism, as the Seagulls are heading for the Europa League under Roberto De Zerbi.

Early on, Solly March waltzes through the Hammers' defence to test Areola and it looks ominous. West Ham hold out for eighteen minutes before Johnson gets under a ball he should head away. The speedy Kaoru Mitoma is on to it instantly, and Bowen brings the winger down with a foolish push in the back when Mitoma still had Aguerd to beat. World Cup winner Mac Allister dispatches the penalty in front of us.

West Ham nearly equalise as Benrahma's run is halted by Estupiñán and the ball rebounds nicely for Bowen, who rounds Adam Webster but shoots against the legs of Jason

Steele. But that's about it from the Hammers. Brighton continue to dominate with everything going through the impressive Moisés Caicedo in midfield, though it remains 1–0 at half-time.

A chant of 'Oh Saïd Benrahma!' goes up from the away fans when Benrahma is predictably hooked by Moyes at half-time, followed by, 'You don't know what you're doing!' Benrahma had at least been involved in setting up the chance for Bowen before the break, even if he is sometimes lacking defensively.

The mood turns more mutinous as Brighton win a corner. Mac Allister flicks it on and Joël Veltman is completely unmarked in the box to chest home a ridiculously easy goal. Johnson is seemingly play-writing rather than man-marking, and Areola hasn't organised his defence to mark the free man.

We just can't get the ball off Brighton, and Souček and co. look like rigid table footballers as Brighton play it out from the back and bypass our men. Even Rice looks mesmerised as he and Souček are both booked for late tackles born of frustration. Soon it's 3–0 as the desperate Rice goes too far upfield to chase the ball. Brighton ping it around and March finds Groß, who crosses for Mitoma to score, having got beyond a daydreaming Johnson. Johnson looked a great prospect a couple of seasons ago and will hopefully recover from this. But after this performance, he will probably still be wandering around the green fields of Falmer trying to track Mitoma as the *Match of the Day* credits play.

'You're getting sacked in the morning!' goes up from the West Ham fans. 'F**king useless c***s!' is one of the more considered verdicts. Then 'How shit must you be / It's only 3–0!' On the rare occasions West Ham gain possession, chants go up of 'We've got the ball! We've got the ball!' Yet, you have to remember that this is the team that won 4–0 last week. We seem to be back at the flakiness level of the Ron Greenwood and John Lyall eras, winning 4–0 one week, losing 4–0 the next. The fans who go to all the away games have clearly seen enough, though inevitably they might be a more volatile lot than the more sedate fans among the 62,000 home crowd. Social media has made everything more extreme too; the manager is either a genius or an out-of-touch dinosaur. Two years ago, Moyes was being hailed as the 'Moyesiah'.

The Seagulls fans start to give their side an 'Olé!' with every pass. Areola makes a fantastic save to tip Julio Enciso's shot on to the bar. Zouma comes on for the injured Ogbonna to a chorus of boos from the cat-loving home fans. Welbeck also arrives.

'Welbeck always scores against us,' warns Joe. We know what comes next. The defence stands well back from Welbeck, who is given far too much space on the edge of the box and fires into the bottom corner. I'm not sure that Areola should have been beaten from the edge of the box, but he had no protection and has made a number of good saves to keep the score down.

'Can we play you every week?' chant the home fans.

The seats are emptying around us.

'We've seen worse. Do you remember 6–0 at Goodison?' I ask Joe.

'And the 6–0 at Oldham in the rain on a plastic pitch. And that was just the first leg,' he reflects.

The advantage of being an older fan is that you become something of a connoisseur of debacles. I always think you should stay to the end, whatever the result. The younger fans who have ostentatiously flounced out of their seats are now standing in the concourse, which doesn't achieve much.

This has been a terrible performance where no one has won their one-versus-one battles, and Brighton, who have played really well, have been made to look like Real Madrid. It should have been quite an attacking side on paper. But with Paquetá and Benrahma out-muscled and Rice and Souček bypassed, plus Ings isolated up front, it's been about as effective as Boris Johnson's Partygate defence. West Ham remain two points above the drop zone.

'Well, that went well,' I reflect at the final whistle.

'Not very Massive anymore, are we Pete?' says Joe. 'I won't be forgetting my first trip to the Amex for a while.'

We join the queue for the train to Lewes and at least the London train from there isn't too crowded. Joe reflects that there are so many London teams in the Premier League that one normally goes down and it might just be us. 'Look forward to doing it all again soon…' he says, departing at Clapham. 'And hopefully we'll still be in the Premiership.'

Rice is despondent in his post-match interview and as ever, is completely honest:

> Brighton played us off the pitch and made life very difficult for us, and to be fair, that wasn't a performance that was acceptable at all. I know it's a cliché to stand here and say it's not good enough but days like today you have to apologise to the fans because we let them down, we've let the club down. Me as a player, I'm hurting, the lads are hurting. We thought we'd turned the corner in recent weeks … Today to have that result is a real setback … They have a unique way of playing and we just didn't work that out … To be out there, for me it was demoralising to be honest with you.

Moyes tells the BBC, 'I'll definitely take all the responsibility because that's what happens as a manager, but also players need to stand up and be counted. Which I'm sure they will. They're a good group.' He tells Sky, '[There are] not any excuses, they were first to the ball, quicker than us, sharper all over the park. We gave away an awful goal for the penalty.'

When asked if he understands the fans' frustrations, the boss answers:

> Totally, after that performance today. I remember the good times in the last two and a half years; we've been seventh in the Premier League, sixth in the Premier League. We're still in Europe, the semi-final last year in Europe, so there's been a lot of good things done. So you hope that when things aren't going quite so well that you get the backing.

On WhatsApp, Fraser, perhaps sensing a chance to snatch Marcelo Bielsa and his bucket, comments, 'Seven goals conceded in four days. Surely this spells the end of the predictably dismal Moyes era.'

Later that evening, there's a further shock when I'm captured by the *Match of the Day 2* cameras among the few remaining diehards in the away end. Big Joe is just out of shot, and I'm seen muttering some possibly deprecating remarks in front of a mournful geezer in a flat cap and rows of empty blue seats. 'West Ham's biggest defeat of the season. Brighton brilliant. West Ham woeful,' intones the commentator.

Jacob Steinberg, who normally knows his stuff, dusts off his 'West Ham in crisis' article and writes in *The Guardian*:

> Although Moyes has not lost the support of the hierarchy, his tactics are causing unease in the dressing room. It is understood some players have grown weary of his caution and feel it is holding them back. There is an increasing lack of faith in the approach favoured by Moyes, who has had little

success with attempts to introduce a more attacking style this season.

You can't really blame the manager for Johnson's nightmare at Brighton but it is worrying if the players are questioning his tactics. However, there is surely no point in changing the manager now with no obvious replacement and no transfer window to work in. We have to hope Moyes uses his experience to get us out of trouble – but to keep his job next season, having spent £160 million, he has to give the fans something to be optimistic about from the final twelve matches.

At least there's some cheer on the TV. Watching series two of the excellent *White Lotus* with Nicola, we find an unlikely West Ham cultural reference. Amid all the rich Americans comes a geezer from Essex called Jack. While romancing Tanya's assistant Portia in Sicily, he gets drunk and breaks into a chorus of 'I'm Forever Blowing Bubbles'. Later, we see that he has a Hammers tattoo on his arm. He also says that before coming out to stay in Sicily with his 'uncle' he got himself into a 'dark hole' in England – presumably a reference to supporting the Irons.

It's good to have a European game on Thursday at AEK Larnaca, away from the pressure of the league. The draw for the round of sixteen has been kind, and West Ham have avoided the bigger teams like Lazio, Fiorentina, Nice and

Basel. The Irons are at Larnaca in Cyprus, which is where our pal Gavin got married.

It's a 5.45 p.m. kick-off on BT Sport in chilly London to see the lads in balmy Cyprus. Joe Cole and Carlton Cole get nostalgic about Ayia Napa in the studio and at the stadium, the big news is that Mark Noble is sporting an Essex geezer flat cap.

After the Brighton debacle the Irons start slowly but at least the returning Zouma looks solid at the back. Larnaca are clearly a limited side but the Irons come to life as Benrahma does a mazy dribble into the box to force a save. The breakthrough comes when Benrahma gets in a fine cross and Antonio, who has got between his markers, heads home. It gets even better when he scores a belter by bending it round his defender to find the top corner and make it 2–0.

The second half sees good work from Lanzini, and Benrahma releases Antonio again, only for his shot to strike the inside of the post. The result is never in doubt as the Hammers play within themselves for most of the second half.

Forgotten man Cornet has an interesting cameo, calmly playing his defence out of trouble on the edge of the box then riding a tackle to release Paquetá with a great through ball. With just Kenan Pirić to beat, Paquetá takes too long and allows the keeper to save. Areola makes a good late stop and then it's all over.

It's hard to read too much into this, but there are some good points after Brighton. Downes had a steady game in midfield, Antonio boosted his confidence after his Old Trafford misses, Lanzini looked eager, Zouma and Cornet returned and even Scamacca got thirty-six minutes of football.

So, it's nine wins out of nine in Europe – as Nigel points out, the Hammers currently have more wins in Europe than the Premier League.

For the Aston Villa match it's a Sunday morning dash from Maidenhead (which Matt says has the longest-standing football ground in the country) where Nicola is doing a paddleboard race. She ends up with a medal after doing 8 km in one hour twenty-one minutes, which is one medal more than most West Ham players currently possess.

Gary Lineker has been suspended by the BBC for breaching their social media guidelines after tweeting criticism of Suella Braverman's 'immeasurably cruel' policy on asylum seekers. Meanwhile, at the London Stadium, Matt is maintaining that his social media content does not contain any technical breaches of media guidelines and that he is equally critical of all referees. There is some concern that the social media output of Fraser might contain some anti-Moyes bias, though five years after Burnley, at least he hasn't suggested a pitch invasion.

Nigel's digital season ticket is playing up and refusing him entry so he has to collect a paper ticket from the box office.

Unluckily for him, it works. Meanwhile, Michael has been to see 1960s *Doctor Who* legends Peter Purves and Maureen O'Brien at the Riverside but has not as yet received a Blue Peter badge from Peter.

Zouma starts and Kehrer replaces Johnson. It's Ings against Mings as West Ham start well, with Bowen looking to have the beating of full-back Àlex Moreno. Rice's free kick is prodded wide by Aguerd. The Moroccan defender then finds Bowen with a lovely crossfield ball, Bowen eludes Moreno and crosses for Benrahma to volley wide.

It all seems to be going well until the seventeenth minute. In Villa's first attack, Kehrer stands off Moreno and the full-back whips in a teasing cross. Ollie Watkins gets ahead of Aguerd to head into the ground and over Areola. A glum silence from the home fans greets the goal.

At least the Irons show good character to come back and equalise. Emiliano Martínez claws away a corner to Paquetá whose shot is headed off the line. In the melee, Paquetá is pushed in the back by Leon Bailey. He goes down easily but the contact was there. It's a silly penalty to give away and Benrahma blasts it home in the manner of Ray Stewart and Julian Dicks.

The Hammers regain momentum and Benrahma plays in a fine cross that Zouma should head on target but doesn't. Before the break, the Hammers are indebted to Areola for making a great reaction save to deny Watkins from close in.

The sides look pretty evenly matched, as the second half begins with something of a personal duel between Benrahma and Martínez. After a quality break, Benrahma curls an effort just wide and then sees another long-range effort tipped over by the World Cup-winning keeper. Nigel unleashes his lucky banana in an effort to conjure a goal.

Paquetá has attempted many clever balls – perhaps too clever, for as Lisa points out, he's not playing in a side of Brazilians. He picks up a booking for a late challenge, then gets subbed for Fornals.

Bowen makes another great run down the right to cut back for Fornals, who makes a hash of his shot. Contrary to some media comments, the crowd do attempt to keep the side going. Benrahma has another goal-bound effort foiled by a great block from the geriatric Ashley Young.

Matt comes out with some decidedly non-Biblical terms when Ings is substituted by Cornet in the eighty-sixth minute, rather than Scamacca. Moyes later says that although Scamacca's hold-up play is good, 'we know that his physical data has got to be much better than it is'. If that means Scamacca needs to put himself about more, then you wonder why West Ham paid £30 million for him. Moyes also suggests that Scamacca is not a player to get behind defences.

In Moyes's defence, Cornet is fast and scored nine goals for Burnley last season. Though when Maxwel does get in a one-on-one, his silver hammer lets him down as he messes it up with an extra stepover before being ruled offside.

Villa have brought on Jhon Durán, who proves not to be hungry like the wolf when he shoots straight at wild boy Areola. There's a late scare when Rice dawdles in the area and then clashes with Emi Buendía. There doesn't look enough in it to be a penalty and a big melee ensues as Rice takes issue with Buendía rolling on the ground.

There are a few boos at the final whistle, which are not quite deserved and later overstated by the media, particularly *The Sun* which headlines its match report, 'Hammers booed off as pressure mounts on David Moyes.' It's a definite improvement on the Brighton game. Villa are not a bad side under Unai Emery, Bowen has played really well and with a bit of luck, Benrahma could have had a hat-trick, though as it is he has amassed a Premier League record of ten shots in one game. We wonder if Moyes really has lost it, as he's forgotten to sub Beni.

So, it's off to The Eagle for Spitfire from the fridge and the news that we are out of the drop zone on goal difference. We need to get some wins from somewhere, but though the result was disappointing, there were some reasons for optimism. We've got points in our last four home games – and that's surely going to be the key to survival.

The Thursday night Europa Conference League game

against Larnaca is something of a dead rubber with the Hammers already 2–0 up from the away leg but proves surprisingly enjoyable. Scamacca is back but Moyes is critical of the big man in his pre-match assessment:

> We want our Gianluca back who we had from August to November. The one we have got right now looks slightly different … We want him to be physically working hard for the team, getting in the right goalscoring positions, playing like a 6ft 4in. centre-forward and covering all the ground. That's what we want from him. In the early part of the season we saw that. We haven't seen it since he has come back from his injury in November around the World Cup.

Pre-match in the Best Meze cafe, Matt and Lisa are feeling extravagant and drinking white wine. We're joined by Nigel and Lisa's pals Bob and Dan. The Best's menu goes upmarket at night, so it is falafel, halloumi, mushrooms and chips all round. The sad news for Nigel is that his digital ticket works for once as we join Fraser in the stadium. Michael is away on thespian duties, possibly playing the role of God. We could do with him here.

Scamacca starts after a spell of injuries and gets a good long-distance shot away early on. Then he gets the luck he needed with a tame effort that goes under Pirić. That goal should be good for his confidence, at least.

Fornals hits the bar with a rasping effort. The Irons escape when Larnaca have a goal disallowed by VAR. But the tie is effectively over when they have Gustavo Ledes dismissed for a late tackle on Fornals, even though a sporting Fornals pleads for leniency.

'What sort of number is 99?' asks Nigel, observing the shirt of Larnaca's Nemanja Nikolić.

'It's Cornet who should be wearing 99,' I suggest.

The crowd is younger than usual. Behind us are several squeaky-voiced boys singing 'Antonio! Antonio!', causing us to wonder if our former player Freddie Sears, who always looked to be about thirteen, has been allowed out late.

After the break, Scamacca shoots, Pirić parries and Bowen fires home the rebound. Two minutes later, Bowen gets his head to a Cresswell cross to score a great goal. The Hammers are disrupted by a series of substitutions but it is good to see kids Levi Laing and Potts come on and even better when Mubama diverts Souček's header into the net with a clever finish for his first Hammers goal. It's great to see the elation of Mubama and the happiness of the players for him as he celebrates in our corner. It's strange to be so relaxed at a West Ham game, but a 6–0 aggregate win isn't bad against a limited side. And now we're into the quarter-finals of the Europa Conference League.

A two-week international break ensues, during which Rice scores from close range for England in Italy. A good way for Deccers to respond to some of the recent criticism from pundits such as Graeme Souness. He might be leaving in the summer but he's still been putting in shifts for West Ham. Souness writes in the *Daily Mail* of Rice's defensive midfield role:

> This role is a vital part of any team because in an ideal world, it's multi-dimensional. You are creative, you chip in with goals and you've got a defensive head at all times. If you've got all three of those attributes, you're worth your weight in gold. For me, Rice has just one.

Quite right Graeme, it's not as if Rice will ever command a fee of, say, £105 million.

In the Europa Conference League, West Ham are drawn away to Belgian side Genk in the quarter-finals. Some fans are starting to dream of winning the trophy, but that way madness lies. Though perhaps I am being affected. When my sister suggests a trip to Norfolk on a forthcoming Thursday, I tell her I'd like to steer clear of the quarter-final and semi-final days, and I've made sure no holidays are booked for the date of the final on 7 June. Mind you, I've been avoiding holidaying on FA Cup final day for forty-three years and that hasn't got me very far.

We'll surely mess it up in some way, just as we did in the Europa League last season. West Ham fans are not noted for their Faustian pacts but a number of supporters speculate over whether they would swap relegation for winning the Europa Conference. A surprising number, particularly younger fans who have never seen West Ham United win anything, say they would.

Meanwhile, Nigel, ever the keen reporter, relays a disturbing conversation: 'Talking to two blokes on train: both said it was a "no-brainer" that they'd choose a European cup over staying in the Premier League. One is booking flights to Prague tomorrow… said they got returns to Larnaca for £88.'

Meanwhile *The Guardian* ends the month with an article on nine teams in danger of dropping into the Championship, with West Ham prominent. Will it be relegation or celebration for the claret and blue? It might not be cup fever, but most fans are feeling a little dizzy and disorientated. Even Matt says he would sacrifice survival to see us win a trophy. And in a hostage to fortune, he says we're the away team if we reach the final. Having been lucky enough to see the Hammers win the FA Cup in 1975 and 1980, I'm not so sure. Relegation could see the club enter a long-term decline and be marooned in the Championship for years. Couldn't we just this once make it easy by avoiding relegation and winning the Europa Conference? Or would that be too unlike West Ham?

9

JARROD BOWEN'S ON FIRE

APRIL 2023

Could it be a lucky omen that I've spotted actor Donald Sumpter getting off the Overground at Hackney Wick? If the man who played Rassilon – Lord High President of the High Council of Time Lords in *Doctor Who* – is on our side, then West Ham might just win a six-pointer against bottom-placed Southampton. Sumpter also played a submarine commander besieged by string-vest-wearing aquatic monsters in the original 'Sea Devils' story on *Doctor Who*, though only a true Whovian like Michael would know that.

Inside the stadium, the big news is that at security Matt has been alerted to a bee inside his yellow hoodie. Perhaps it thinks that he is a giant daffodil. Could it be an agent from Brentford? After Lisa successfully places the bee on some vegetation, she suggests that it might have flown off to play for the Bee Team.

It's already been an epic week for Matt, Lisa and Michael who have been to see The Fizz (once Bucks Fizz) at the O2 – the former Eurovision winners being rather like West Ham in letting their indecision take them from behind before making their minds up. We're joined by Nigel (whose digital season ticket is still playing up) and Fraser, plus my old school friend Steve the Cornish postie, who is hoping to improve West Ham's delivery.

The Irons make the obligatory slow start. The players seem nervous as the crowd starts to get on Benrahma's back for playing the ball backwards. Theo Walcott sends a volley wide for the Saints but apart from some fine Rice interceptions, it's pretty tame stuff until Bowen wins a free kick in the twenty-fourth minute. Kehrer swings over a decent free kick and the unmarked Aguerd powers home a header. The ref disallows it for offside before VAR intervenes. You could read most of *War and Peace* in the time it takes to come to a decision, but after three and a half minutes, the goal is given. Aguerd celebrates his first Hammers goal all over again.

There's a scare as Saints come straight back but Roméo Lavia's goal-bound shot is superbly tipped round the post by the returning Fabiański. It's a great reaction save from him. The Hammers almost make it two before the break as Bowen does really well to cut inside two defenders, look up and whack a shot against the crossbar.

At half-time, Nigel is instructed by the rest of us not to eat his lucky banana as we're already winning. The second half sees Southampton have lots of possession without looking too threatening. The Hammers have their moments on the break. Ings is almost released but doesn't have the pace to get beyond the defence, though does find Bowen who fires wide.

When Emerson is fouled on the edge of the area, Benrahma's free kick is tipped round the post by Gavin Bazunu. It's a poor match, but Paquetá is having a good game in midfield doing un-Paquetá-like things, getting stuck in and winning more tackles than any other player on the pitch. Also encouraging is the fact that the centre-back partnership of Aguerd and Zouma looks well balanced and holds firm against the Saints' probing. Kehrer has a decent game at right-back and we avoid giving away any free kicks in James Ward-Prowse territory.

Bazunu has to prevent an own goal by Duje Ćaleta-Car from Bowen's cross. A corner finds Paquetá at the back post but he swivels and volleys over the bar. Antonio comes on for Ings and confuses both his teammates and the opposition, at one point almost smuggling the ball over the line with it seemingly glued to his chest.

The Saints bring on the giant 6 ft 7in. Paul Onuachu who

provides a focal point up front. Urged on by some noisy away support, they almost equalise as Ward-Prowse gets in a good cross and Onuachu plants a header against the bar.

Sub Downes does a good job of holding the ball up and Bowen wastes time on the wing as the Irons see out three minutes of added time. Not pretty, but the result is everything.

Matt and Lisa head off to watch the West Ham women's team play at Dagenham. This makes it four games in two days for uber-fan Lisa, who has also seen the Under-18s and the Under-21s play on Saturday. Perhaps she could fit in a 7.45 p.m. kick-off as well?

The rest of us head to The Eagle where Fraser is treated to table service as we try not to remind him that Moyes has escaped the sack again. On the TV we learn that Brendan Rodgers at Leicester has indeed been sacked. There are rumours that Graham Potter will soon depart Chelsea too. Perhaps they should appoint Frank Lampard again, we joke.

The Saints remain bottom and West Ham go up to fourteenth. To be positive, that's five league games at home unbeaten. Hopefully this result will give the side some confidence to play more expansively and get some kind of result against third-placed Newcastle on Wednesday.

Bad news arrives on the injury front as the *Daily Mail* reports that Scamacca is out with a knee injury and might need surgery. The big Italian arrived with great expectations but is now enduring hard times.

Wednesday night's home match against Newcastle is not a great game to take my two daughters to, though I'm sure the therapy bills will lessen, and my own PTSD might ease at some point. Lola is down from Edinburgh for the week, and Nell is back at home with us and now working as a learning support assistant at a school in Barnet. Sorting out a pair of tickets costs £100 but what does that matter when my daughters are about to see West Ham beat the Sportswashers?

Michael is away on theatrical duties, but we're joined by Fraser, Matt, Lisa, Nigel and his groundhopping pal Reg's son Henry, who appears to have morphed into Kurt Cobain. We're definitely searching for something that smells like team spirit. In the first minute, Bowen makes a great run into the box and his low cross is poked on to his own post by Guimarães. The crowd are up for it under the lights.

But then the Hammers are behind after Newcastle's first attack. Kehrer gives away a needless corner, Benrahma fails to close down Saint-Maximin and Wilson climbs between Zouma and Aguerd to head home. Terrible marking there. On twelve minutes, Schär's simple through ball sees Joelinton get round the back of Kehrer and score. VAR intervenes but Joelinton's been played onside by Emerson (and probably Lake and Palmer too).

The Hammers show some character to come back. Nick Pope makes a good save from Paquetá's free kick and Sven Botman makes a great block to deny Antonio, who also has a decent penalty appeal turned down. The Irons pull one back when Pope gets under Bowen's corner and Zouma heads home.

Nigel eats his lucky banana at half-time, and we hope it's going to be a tight game after Zouma's goal. That mood lasts for twenty-three seconds. We're just taking our seats as Fabiański throws the ball out to Aguerd who is in a difficult position and being pressed. Aguerd miscontrols horribly, Jacob Murphy nicks it and presents Wilson with a simple tap in.

Moyes brings on four subs but the game is effectively over. Another Sunday league goal arrives when Fabiański, who has made three decent saves to keep the score down, rushes from goal only to nudge the ball to Alexander Isak, who lobs the fourth.

The seats around us are either empty or full of vicars' sons hurling abuse at our defensive miscreants. As added time arrives, Paquetá loses the ball and Joelinton beats two defenders to fire home the fifth. 'You're getting sacked in the morning!' sing the away and a few home fans.

So, it's home for a stiff whisky and a counselling session in the morning. Whatever Moyes is doing it isn't working, and the new signings have backfired. My hunch is he'll be given the Fulham game to save his job. Newcastle look a good side under Howe but if West Ham defend like this, we're going down. However, it's not Moyes doing the defending – professionals should be able to eliminate such basic mistakes, and the players need to respond at Craven Cottage.

Speaking after the match, Moyes is, as always, honest and concedes he might be close to the sack: 'I'm a big boy; I've left jobs at other times in the past and if that happens, I'll have to go with that. But I really like my job here.'

With West Ham only out of the bottom three on goal difference, *The Guardian*'s Jacob Steinberg tweets, 'A real sense David Moyes could be sacked if West Ham lose at Fulham tomorrow. But the lack of an obvious replacement means it isn't a guarantee.'

West Ham and Nottingham Forest remain the only two clubs in the bottom half of the league not to have sacked their managers, which says something about the panic-riddled lower reaches of the Premiership.

In the *Daily Mail*, Lewis Steele describes Moyes's position as 'untenable' and says that the fanbase 'has given up on their manager'. He concludes:

> A team criticised so much for being too defensive has seemingly forgotten how to defend. Playing like that, you could imagine any team turning up and beating West Ham. Managers are not sacked on one performance alone but this thumping defeat whiffed of the sort that could lead a hierarchy to act.

On my blog, a fan called Phil comments:

> David Sullivan and David Moyes are like Thelma and Louise driving West Ham over a cliff. This is now gross negligence by Sullivan and I can't help but think that he's being stubborn in not sacking Moyes. A new interim manager could get the new coach bounce and gain some good results for West Ham. Giving Moyes yet another game is madness, because if we lose it's over and if we win we'll still get smashed by the juggernauts still to come.

So, after the Everton and Nottingham Forest matches comes another must-win game at Fulham. Perhaps in desperation, Moyes reverts to many of the players who did so well to get the side to sixth place during the lockdown season of 2020–21. Cresswell replaces Emerson at left-back and Coufal comes in for Kehrer at right-back. Aguerd is dropped for Ogbonna and Fornals comes into midfield to replace the injured Paquetá. And astonishingly, Moyes plays two strikers, in the form of Antonio and Ings. On WhatsApp, I wonder if this is a late bid to win over Fraser. It's a workmanlike team of scrappers, featuring none of the summer signings. The team is going back to the formula that initially helped West Ham survive and then reach sixth place.

It's a nervous trip to the Lake District for myself while the scores from this one are updated, though that might be a lucky omen as the last time the Irons won while I was on the road I was also heading to the Lakes, back in late August.

We still can't score, but at least Fulham do it for us. The goal comes when a Coufal cross is half-cleared and falls to Bowen. His low cross is turned into his own net by the heel of Fulham's Harrison Reed. 'Bless Fulham for gifting us an own goal,' comments Fraser on WhatsApp.

From then on, it's a resilient defensive performance reminiscent of the West Ham of two seasons ago with Ogbonna prominent. On the break, Bowen sets up Ings for a shot, which is smothered by Leno.

When Ings is subbed for Downes it provokes a chorus of 'You don't know what you're doing!' from the away fans, who clearly haven't forgiven Moyes for the Brighton performance. Only, perhaps he does know what he's doing, as the arrival of subs Downes and Benrahma gives Fulham something else to think about.

The Irons rely on a great late dive from Fabiański to tip the ball away from Pereira, who is through on goal and trying to round the keeper. It should be 2–0 in added time, but sub Cornet opts to shoot rather than pass to the unmarked Benrahma.

At the end of a hard-earned away victory, some West Ham fans in the away end still hold up a 'Moyes Out' banner, which isn't necessary when we've won and forgets all the good work Moyes has done at the club. He's a decent man and deserves better. West Ham go up to the heights of thirteenth place on thirty points, and another three wins out of the final nine games should see the side survive.

It's three very valuable away points, though also a victory that raises questions as the team played better without the new signings. But with two wins out of the last three games, it makes the reaction of the last week seem rather melodramatic. The gaffer describes it as 'a great bounce back' and dismisses the Newcastle game as a freak result, pointing out the side has two clean sheets in a week. 'We'd like to be playing better … [but you have to] find a way of getting your results.'

For most of the season, European matches have come as something of a relief after the pressure in the league. A bit like in *Withnail and I* we seem to have reached a European quarter-final by mistake.

I watch the away leg against KAA Gent on BT Sport via my laptop while still in Keswick, having bagged my 214th and final Wainwright fell in the Lake District after forty-odd years of walking in the Lakes. The day after my triumph, a group of walkers – high in all senses, on magic mushrooms – have to be helped off the fells by the Keswick mountain rescue team. This causes some speculation in the West Ham WhatsApp group that it might have been me and my support team over-celebrating.

For the Gent game, Moyes has to rotate again with Arsenal coming up on Sunday. His five-man defence doesn't really work, with Emerson in particular looking unsure of his position, but thankfully Gent waste chances in front of a passionate crowd.

Aguerd has a goal disallowed for handball after capitalising on a goalkeeping clanger. But the Irons do take the lead before the break. A quick throw-in catches out the home defence and from Bowen's low cross, Ings scores a simple tap-in – his first ever goal in Europe at thirty years old.

The second half sees Gent come at the Hammers, and they equalise after the defence fails to track the runners and Hugo Cuypers sweeps home. Bowen misses a decent chance, while Gift Orban almost scores for Gent with a great overhead kick. The game ends with a cancelled red card after the ref rules that sub Paquetá was in fact tackled fairly on the edge of the area.

It's going to be a tight second leg. It's the first game the Hammers haven't won in Europe this season, which is testament to the raised expectations created by Moyes. It's not a bad result to draw the away leg at Gent, but Mystic Matt is maybe having a bad day in London and is particularly agitated online, declaring:

> Moyes picked a baffling formation the players didn't understand and failed to change it until they scored, leaving Rice to try to sort it out. Downes and Johnson were miles off the pace, Emerson clearly didn't know where he was supposed to

> be playing and Lanzini never got going. Against the best team we have played, Moyes totally blew it. Play like this against Arsenal and we will lose 6–0.

I wonder if he might like some of my magic mushrooms from the Lake District to help him cope with the Arsenal game.

The Gunners arrive at the London Stadium top of the league but having just dropped two points at Anfield. I arrive at Hackney Wick with a feeling we might just upset Arsenal today. Matty Etherington is on the pitch pre-match, and I'm joined by Matt, Lisa, Nigel, Fraser and Michael at a spring-like London Stadium. Kehrer is in for the injured Ogbonna and Paquetá returns after injury. Scamacca is about to have a knee operation, ending his troublesome first season.

But it all seems to be going very wrong after ten minutes as another Newcastle-style thrashing beckons. First, Ben White gets behind the home defence and crosses for Gabriel Jesus to tap home. *Match of the Day 2* fingers Benrahma for not tracking back but Cresswell, Kehrer and Coufal are also caught off-guard. It's 2–0 when Martinelli plays in a teasing cross for the unmarked Ødegaard to drift in and stroke home.

The Arsenal fans get decidedly cocky, singing 'You're going down!' and 'Are you Tottenham in disguise?', but they don't realise West Ham have a new continental midfielder called *Schadenfreude*.

Arsenal ease off and something happens after West Ham

remember to compete. The Gunners' defenders don't like it when Antonio runs at them. On thirty-three minutes, West Ham are right back in it. Rice dispossesses a dawdling Partey and feeds Paquetá. He feels contact from Gabriel and goes down in the box to win a penalty. Benrahma sends Ramsdale the wrong way from the spot to score.

The crowd is ignited again as Benrahma makes a storming run from his own half to win a free kick. Antonio heads the resulting cross into the ground, and Ramsey has to tip the bouncing ball over. Jesus starts to lose his cool and gets petulant. The Irons play a lot better, and Arsenal look worried. At half-time, Nigel eats his lucky banana, as it's all to play for at 2–1 down.

The Irons win a couple of early corners but then the game seems over as Antonio turns his back on the ball in his own box and the ball strikes his hand. Penalty to Arsenal. Saka takes a short run-up and strikes the ball somewhere towards the River Lee, to much derision from the Hammers' fans.

That inspires both the crowd and the players. Kehrer lofts a ball back into the Arsenal box and there is Bowen to expertly volley down into the ground and up over a flailing Ramsdale as the stadium erupts. 'Jarrod Bowen's on fire and he's shagging Dani Dyer! Der der der der, der, der, der, der! Ooh!' sing the crowd to the tune of 'Freed From Desire'. A more feminist version of this anthem might be 'Dani Dyer's on fire and she's shagging Jarrod Bowen!' but sadly this doesn't scan.

Those Gunners fans are not singing anymore. The Lego-like figure of Mikel Arteta looks he's about to come apart in his technical area.

It's turned into a really good game that could go either way. Coufal has a fine match and makes one great tackle on Martinelli, while Paquetá is busy and effective in midfield and Antonio and Bowen are causing all sorts of problems running at the Arsenal back line.

Arsenal go close when Jesus just fails to connect with a cross, and Bowen does really well to head away a dangerous Saka cross from on the line. Saka can only shoot straight at Fabiański when released after a poor Paquetá pass. Benrahma shows fine determination to outmuscle Rob Holding and get in a swinging cross that Antonio heads against the angle of post and bar. So, it's nearly a famous comeback from 2–0 down.

We have five minutes of nervous added time to get through as 'Come on you Irons!' sounds around the stadium but ultimately, it's a great bonus point that gives Man City the upper hand in the title race – at least until we win at the Etihad. And some big performances from Paquetá, Antonio and Bowen.

We head off to The Eagle in a jovial mood. As we watch Forest lose, Nigel tells us about his forthcoming Zombies gig and how Colin Blunstone quit music for a couple of years to become an accountant. Matt receives preferential treatment as he is presented with an East London Pale Ale from the mysterious contents of The Eagle's fridge, Michael chats with a fan of his plays at the bar and Fraser celebrates the survival of Moyes yet again with an alcohol-free Guinness.

In the post-match interviews, Arsenal's Arteta says that 'instead of killing them we gave them hope', which sounds a little extreme even for a London derby. Moyes praises his three midfield players and says Bowen is 'getting back to it … his goal was typical Jarrod, hoping to get in, hoping to get a chance to score and when he got the one, he took it'. He thinks the result is a big psychological boost.

A satisfying day all round and another win or so should see West Ham survive, with the bottom five seeming to be in real trouble. In a troubled season, this is only the second point we've taken off one of the top four.

Thursday evening sees the second leg of the Europa Conference League quarter-final against KAA Gent. I'm joined by Nigel and his wife Carolyn, Fraser, Sinead from The Eagle (wearing a West Ham/Gent half-and-half scarf that is the envy of Nigel and Matt) and Matt and Lisa. Michael is away, spending more time with his West Ham cushions and Jonathan Spector shirt on stage at the White Bear Theatre.

Moyes has picked a strong side, sensing that winning the Europa Conference League is the best way of keeping his job. West Ham start brightly, with Emerson testing the keeper but soon start to look nervous as Orban misses a close-range header for Gent. Coufal goes down after a worrying clash of heads, but eventually the RoboCop plays on.

The Belgians play some neat football in front of their bouncing away crew and take the lead after a series of errors. Paquetá gives away a simple ball in midfield, Orban scuffs over a cross, Matisse Samoise mishits it to Cuypers, who also scuffs his shot. The ball is chested over his own line by Aguerd when he should surely have headed it away.

The Gent fans start to flash their mobiles seemingly in the fashion of a Killers concert, though we later learn it's a tribute to a singer from Gent who died at the age of fifty-two. It all looks worrying until West Ham win a free kick on the right. Bowen whips it in, and Antonio gets across his marker to power home a header.

At half-time, Mystic Matt says we've played three halves against Gent and looked worse in all of them, and he can see us losing. A quick straw poll sees Nigel predicting a home defeat, Fraser opting for penalties and optimists Lisa and myself going for 3–2 and 2–1 wins respectively.

But we have reckoned without the power of confectionary. Nigel eschews eating his lucky banana, but Sinead is passing round some lucky gums that soon work some magic. West Ham start the second half with purpose. Souček clatters Bowen's cross against the angle of post and bar and Bowen then draws a good safe from Davy Roef.

The key moment comes when defender Joseph Okumu

stumbles, with his hand hitting the ball for an obvious penalty. Strangely, the ref waves play on and Antonio hits the post. After a long melee, eventually VAR is called upon and after several millennia, the penalty is given. For some reason, Benrahma doesn't take it. Instead, Paquetá takes a stuttering run-up, does a little hop, skip and jump and steers it past Roef, having sent him the wrong way.

That was cool, though we all imagine how irate our old pal Denis (who is still trying to forgive Di Canio for his 'poncy penalty' against Villa twenty-five years ago) would have been had he missed. The away fans are taunted by the rest of the stadium turning on their phone torches and waving them in the air. You're not flashing anymore.

Something is stirring as the crowd gets noisy. Rice wins a tackle in his own half, gets the ball back from Paquetá and rampages down the pitch. Antonio has distracted a couple of defenders and Rice shimmies round a couple more, runs into the box and steers home a low left-foot shot. Moyes does a dad dance in celebration of a fantastic goal. For the first time in ages 'West Ham are massive! Everywhere we go!' echoes around the London Stadium. There can't be many football chants inspired by The Beautiful South but this one is a reworking of the song 'Rotterdam'.

West Ham are intimidating the Gent defence effectively. Three minutes later, Paquetá feeds Antonio who runs at the Gent defence down the left channel. He cuts inside and curls a corker into the top of the net. 'If Antonio hadn't scored the first goal, he wouldn't have got the second,' says Matt. This is what a confident Antonio can do, much more like the striker of two years ago.

There's still time for Bowen to have a fifth goal disallowed and for Matt to come out with some ungodly language as sub Cornet fluffs a chance when set free. Rice, Zouma and Antonio go off with Bournemouth in mind as the Irons cruise to their second European semi-final in two seasons. It's not as prestigious as the Europa League but after forty-three years, we'll take any trophy going. Suddenly, the season isn't looking so bad.

We retire to Ye Olde Black Bull for a pint of Ringwood Razor Back and we watch Maguire and de Gea mess up in the Europa League as Man United lose in Seville. Maybe our run will get some more attention now United are out of Europe. Walking to the tube, we wonder if West Ham could join the Europa Conference full time instead of the Premier League and develop a fierce rivalry with Larnaca, Gent and AZ Alkmaar.

Granted, we should beat possibly the best team in the Belgian league on money spent but this was still one of the best nights of the season and more like the old West Ham. Hopefully, it will also inspire confidence for the six-pointer at Bournemouth.

The week is rounded off by a visit to see Michael's play *A*

Certain Term at the White Bear Theatre in Oval. He is perhaps the greatest playwright to be associated with West Ham since Ben Johnson. Michael's play is particularly memorable for a set containing a seat from the Boleyn Ground, a West Ham cushion and a Jonathan Spector shirt, perhaps providing the Spector at the feast.

Sunday's match at the Vitality Stadium should be a tough one. But for once it's an enjoyable experience listening to a West Ham away game on Radio London. It's a perfect start when after five minutes a loosely marked Antonio heads home Cresswell's corner. It gets even better after twelve minutes when Coufal crosses and Paquetá heads home. What we didn't expect from the Brazilian was bullet headers and tough tackling but that's what we are getting, as he continues to adapt to the English league.

Meanwhile, the stat that Nigel has repeated all season about us being the only team never to have scored in the first fifteen minutes has been well and truly busted. Bournemouth have a good spell where Jefferson Lerma and Solanke test Fabiański, but the game is over just before half-time when another corner drops to Rice, who smashes it home. Astonishing. At half-time, an emergency beep sounds on my phone, presumably a mayday message from Spurs who have let in five goals in twenty-one minutes at Newcastle. It turns out it's the government testing an emergency alert service.

The second half sees West Ham containing the Cherries

before Bowen crosses and Fornals scores with a brilliant scorpion kick. He's in tears after scoring, presumably in shock at West Ham scoring four goals away from home. 'Are you Tottenham in disguise?' ask the Irons fans, followed by a request to Declan for 'ten more years playing football the West Ham way'. Sub Cornet seems to score a fifth 'goal', only to be correctly ruled offside.

The side have taken a lot of confidence from the draw against Arsenal and the win against Gent, and this is quite an achievement after Thursday's exertions with mainly the same players – and against a Bournemouth side that was doing well under former West Ham player Gary O'Neil. From 0–4 at Brighton to 4–0 at Bournemouth. This sees the Hammers almost out of the relegation dogfight on thirty-four points, and another win should see us completely safe. Nigel is particularly pleased that For-nals made it four-nil.

I seem to be emulating Lisa by attending two games in two days the following week. On Tuesday night, it's a very enjoyable trip to the Emirates Stadium for the FA Youth Cup final between Arsenal and West Ham. The tickets are only £5, and it's a great turnout of 7,000 West Ham fans in the Clock End for this Under-18s final. The gate of 34,127 isn't bad for a kids' game.

I'm with daughter Nell and sitting a couple of rows behind diehards Matt and Lisa. The Hammers line-up includes

Mubama and Scarles who have both played for the first team this season.

Keeper Mason Terry has to make a great save from a free kick early on, and Arsenal take the lead when Omari Benjamin finishes well after a Terry save falls to him on the edge of the box. But this young West Ham side don't seem to realise they are meant to lose at the Emirates. George Earthy makes a forceful run from midfield, gets a slightly lucky rebound and scores with a thumping shot. A few minutes later, Callum Marshall gets on the end of an inviting cross to make it 2–1.

The half ends on a high as captain Gideon Kodua pounces on some defensive dithering to score with an excellent thirty-yard chip over the keeper. It's quiet in the library, apart from in the West Ham end where the chants jukebox is going through 'Bubbles', 'West Ham are massive!' and 'My name is Luděk Mikloško / I come from near Moscow…'

The second half sees sustained Arsenal pressure thwarted by determined blocks from Kaelan Casey and co. and some fine saves from Terry. Having soaked up the Arsenal onslaught, West Ham win a corner when Earthy's shot is saved. Casey heads home from the set-piece and is mobbed under a pile of players. It's five goals when sub Joshua Briggs scores with his first shot. A chant of 'You're getting sacked in the morning!' is cheekily directed at Gunners Under-18s boss Jack Wilshere.

At the end, the PA is forced to play 'Bubbles' and it's moving to see these young players celebrate the best moment of their fledgling careers. Gaffer Kevin Keen comes on the pitch and gets a deserved chant from the fans. And then there's the unexpected sight of a West Ham team lifting a trophy.

It's too early to say whether any of this group will emulate 1999 FA Youth Cup winners Michael Carrick and Joe Cole but on this showing, the Irons have some great prospects coming up. And it's not often we win 5–1 at the Emirates. So that's the first trophy of the season won. Surely, we can't win another?

The following evening, it's back to the London Stadium for the Liverpool match where Nigel is enjoying listening to 'The Trooper' by Iron Maiden and is still in disbelief that his new digital season ticket is actually working. He's with Big Sam, the son of his wife Carolyn's oldest friend, and we're joined by regulars Matt, Lisa and Fraser.

Early on, Liverpool's Alisson, whose aim is not true, passes straight to Bowen and his cross almost finds Antonio. Mohamed Salah has a shot blocked at the other end. The Hammers take the lead with a fine goal. It starts with some great control from Benrahma and then sees an intricate one-two between Antonio and Paquetá before the Brazilian unleashes a screamer from the edge of the box. It's a brilliant goal. Now that looks like the work of a £50 million player and underlines Paquetá's recent improvement.

The crowd is full of noise and positivity, and it looks like we might upset the Scousers. They are pinging it around well though, with Trent Alexander-Arnold moving from right-back into central midfield for much of the game. It's Alexander-Arnold who finds Cody Gakpo twenty-five yards from goal. The Liverpool striker is not closed down quickly enough and fires a hard, low shot in off the post.

Diego Jota goes close with a couple of chances for Liverpool but West Ham match them. With Jordan Henderson filling in at right-back at times, Antonio causes him problems. Benrahma gets down the left to cross across the box and only a last-ditch intervention from Virgil van Dijk prevents Antonio from scoring. From the corner, Rice wins the first header but Antonio can't direct the second header on target.

The second half sees the Irons apparently take the lead. A great through ball from Aguerd releases Bowen who races into the box, stands up van Dijk and, with very little backlift, fires into the net. Only sodding VAR intervenes and he's offside by a boot. This proves costly, as West Ham's zonal marking at a corner is all wrong and Joël Matip crashes home a free header.

West Ham make a determined effort to equalise, and the key moment is when Thiago tries to tackle sub Ings and falls on the ball with his hand. Astonishingly, ref Chris Kavanagh doesn't even consult VAR. Moyes gives the officials his Glasgow death stare and later makes a valid point that if the defender lunges in and is out of control it should be a penalty, even if the handball was accidental.

There's still time for Matt the vicar's son to berate Ings for bottling a challenge with Alisson, and for him to berate Cornet for being Cornet, before Liverpool end up winning their third game in succession. They looked more like the Liverpool of old tonight, so it's no disgrace to lose to them. It's been an entertaining match, however. Aguerd made some great interceptions and Paquetá looked like he's now a Premier League force, so there are reasons for optimism.

We head off to Ye Olde Black Bull, where an angry and shouty punter has to be ejected – and it's not David Moyes. On the TV, Arsenal are getting battered by Man City as Nigel and Matt engage in some competitive groundhopping tales and discuss players with palindromic names like Eze. The Brixton Pale Ale is a bonus, though once we see the replay of Thiago's handball it's back to berating officialdom. Still, on this form West Ham should hopefully get some survival points from the next six games.

West Ham have played nine matches in April, and by the time they play their final game of the month at Crystal Palace, the side looks very tired. It's a game that is live on BT Sport at 12.30. The kick-off is delayed by fifteen minutes thanks to dodgy season ticket readers, and in the first half it seems West Ham's defence might have failed to get in to Selhurst Park too.

It's a great start – another goal in the first fifteen minutes for the Irons when Olise heads a corner across his own box and Souček slams home for his first league goal since August.

But then there's a defensive collapse. Zouma isn't quite tight enough on Ayew who slots home with a good finish. He is then injured trying to tackle and goes off to be replaced by Ogbonna. While the defence is regrouping, a cross from Emerson's flank isn't cut out and Zaha mishits home, having got away from Coufal at the far post.

Roy Hodgson has come back at the age of seventy-five to do a really good job at Palace. The Hammers just can't cope with the flair of Eze, Olise and Zaha, aided by the team play of Ayew, and concede a catastrophic third. Aguerd foolishly gives the ball to Souček in a dangerous position. Souček has his pocket picked by Jeffrey Schlupp, who calmly slots it past Fabiański.

At least the Irons keep at it and pull one back from another corner. Souček flicks on and Antonio heads in at the back stick.

At the break, Moyes brings on Benrahma and Cresswell for Fornals and Emerson, though the Hammers never get any passing going in midfield. The extra day's rest Palace have had proves crucial. Palace go 4–2 up with a dodgy penalty scored by Eze. Aguerd's arm was out but he barely touched Eze.

West Ham only ever look like scoring from a corner, and sure enough, Souček gets his head to another corner and his looping header is just about turned in by Aguerd. An eventful afternoon for Souček who has scored one goal and made three assists, two for West Ham and one for Palace.

There are eight minutes of added time but Palace deserve the points, and Benrahma's final wayward cross sums up the afternoon. It's obviously disappointing to score three goals away from home and lose.

But progress has been made in April. One more win should see the Hammers safe, and the side has reached another European semi-final. Could it be time to start dreaming?

10

THE FINAL COUNTDOWN

MAY 2023

May begins with a predictable away defeat to champions-elect Manchester City. It's the worst possible preparation for the Irons, with the news that Zouma is probably out for several weeks and Rice, Souček and Aguerd have succumbed to a bug in the Hammers' camp.

The revamped side gives a decent defensive performance in the goalless first half. Fabiański has to make a smart save from Riyad Mahrez and Rodri hits the post after a give and go with Haaland. But Ogbonna has been getting his head on everything, and Downes is solid enough as the only defensive midfielder. On the left, Paquetá and Emerson have combined well at times. West Ham even nearly score when Bowen gets away down the right and fires at Stefan Ortega. A cross to Emerson might have seen a tap-in.

But with so much possession, City's pressure tells in the second half. Downes gives away a foul in a bad area and from the free kick Nathan Aké heads home, with Ogbonna having played the City strikers onside by getting back too early.

Coufal goes off with a pulled hamstring, and the Hammers bring on Ben Johnson. It's two when sub Ings loses possession. Grealish breaks and plays through Haaland, who beats Fabiański with a delicate chip for his record-breaking thirty-fifth goal of the Premier League season. On this form, he'd probably get in our team. If only City had a decent manager like Leeds's new interim boss Big Sam Allardyce who is apparently as good as Guardiola, at least in his own estimation.

A deflected strike from Foden makes it 3–0. Late on, Paquetá gets through to see a shot parried by Ortega. It's no disgrace to lose at City but the Hammers now have an injury and illness crisis and need to get something from the last four games to be safe.

Sunday sees a difficult home game against Manchester United, who are challenging for a Champions League spot in the top four. This is West Ham's fifty-first match of the season.

It's surely a lucky omen when Michael buys his first ever programme, enticed by the prospect of six pages on American idol Jonathan Spector, the only West Ham player ever to read the *Financial Times*.

It's a strange Sunday evening kick-off at 7 p.m. but inside the stadium the atmosphere is cracking, and Nigel's season ticket has worked for two games running. We're joined by Fraser, sporting a Big Sam-style tan after a scouting trip to Portugal, plus Matt and Lisa.

West Ham start off with some early attacks, but United threaten on the break through Rashford's speed. Bruno Fernandes drags a shot narrowly wide, then so does Antony, while Rashford cuts inside to graze the post. This looks ominous.

Yet, West Ham take the lead when Benrahma escapes Luke Shaw close to the centre circle and races into the United half. He has three players around him but makes ground with a surging run and then fires off a fairly tame shot that looks an easy gather for the keeper. But de Gea goes down like a fallen conifer and can only help Beni's rocket into the net. The crowd celebrates in disbelief. Nigel says it's always worth hoping for a fumble (and he's got some opinions on shooting, too).

Antony shoots against the outside of the post soon after but the Hammers remain reassuringly resilient. Rice is everywhere and Kehrer is having a solidly aggressive game at right-back, while Antonio's strength is causing problems for the United defence. Just before the break, the Irons are denied a penalty when, after de Gea saves from Benrahma, Victor Lindelöf handles – in fact, juggles – in the box. In the current climate, it should surely have been given but the ref ignores the appeal.

At half-time, Fraser and I predict a 1–0 home win, though a pessimistic Nigel goes for a United victory. The second half sees West Ham make a determined effort to get a second goal, with Paquetá increasingly influential. Souček stings the palms of de Gea with a shot.

'West Ham are massive!' chants the crowd. From Kehrer's long throw, Antonio and de Gea go up for the ball. The keeper falls to the ground and Antonio hooks home. The goal is disallowed, though replays show there's not too much wrong with it – Antonio's arm brushes de Gea but it's hard to believe this would be a foul against an outfield player.

Next, after good work from Benrahma, Paquetá crosses and Souček volleys into the side netting. Another Paquetá cross sees Souček head home, only for the goal to be disallowed as he is just offside.

United look tired after playing on Thursday but make a determined effort to snatch a point. Fabiański has to make a fine tip over to deny Rashford. The keeper then palms away an effort from sub Anthony Martial. On seventy-five minutes, Matt and Nigel debate what other entertainment form sees you paying large sums of money but wanting it to be over as quickly as possible.

Souček is injured defending a corner but bravely plays on. Someone once said of him, 'He's the sort of player who would head a fridge.' There's a nerve-wracking eight minutes of injury time as huge choruses of 'I'm Forever Blowing Bubbles' waft over the London Stadium.

Moyes makes good use of time-wasting substitutions, bringing on Fornals, Downes, Johnson and Emerson. There's an almighty scare as Fernandes's corner is headed across the six-yard box by Martial.

Downes does well to get the ball into the corner in the ninth (ninth!) minute of added time. Finally, the whistle blows and Moyes is on the pitch hugging Rice, who has driven the side on all game. It is Moyes's first league win against United since they sacked him in 2014.

We have time to make it to The Eagle for some bottles of East London Pale Ale, where favourite customer Fraser is treated to quiche and chips. Matt even has some top trivia about Joe Hart winning every English and Scottish trophy, asking which other players have done the same (the answer is Kenny Dalglish and Andrei Kanchelskis).

Thirty-seven points should be enough. Apart from a victory against United's second-string side in the Carabao Cup, Moyes has never before beaten his old club. He is beaming in the post-match interview:

> I felt like clapping my own owners because there were times this year when they could have made a change … and I felt like applauding them for how well they were to stick with me

> at different times this season … I thought the crowd were fantastic but no wonder the way the players played tonight … the character the players showed, the passion the players showed … We put on a really good show.

This is more like it – West Ham under the lights and the crowd playing a huge part in victory. Barring a set of miraculous results from Leeds, Everton, Leicester and Forest the Hammers are now staying up and can concentrate on trying to get to a European final.

The games keep coming. Sunday's win against United is followed by the Thursday Europa Conference League tie against AZ Alkmaar. It's a full-scale programme disaster. Despite arriving through the security barrier from Hackney Wick at 7.20 p.m., our group finds the programmes have sold out. Matt, Lisa, Michael, Carolyn and Nigel have found the same thing at the Stratford gates. Only Fraser, the Fonz of programme collectors, has somehow managed to do a deal to secure one.

We're treated to a mosaic of plastic squares reading 'Irons', plus flamethrowers and fireworks, before kick-off in front of a noisy crowd, most of whom appear to have had a sniff of the barmaid's apron. There's an air of desperate expectancy among the Hammers fans. Billy Beane, who features in Michael Lewis's book *Moneyball* and has a minority stake in

Alkmaar, is in the crowd to view his side against opponents West Ham – probably the least *Moneyball* club in football.

The Irons start well, with Antonio's pace and Benrahma's dribbling testing the Alkmaar defence and Benrahma doing well to get in a quick shot that Matt Ryan tips past the post. But it's also clear that former Brighton keeper Ryan and his defenders are going to waste as much time as possible, and Alkmaar are a decent passing side capable of slowing the game down. The ref is not giving Antonio anything after some of his more theatrical falls, and the official makes some bizarre and fussy decisions that annoy the crowd.

The Hammers go behind after forty-one minutes. The players are distracted, claiming for a foul after Paquetá appears to be pushed, and allow Alkmaar to break. Souček doesn't come out quickly enough to close down Tijjani Reijnders, who fires home a shot from outside the box that catches out Areola. Are West Ham going to blow another semi-final?

The atmosphere turns even more febrile, with some angry Herberts behind us moaning about every misplaced pass. If only they could be more positive like my pal Matt. Michael is tempted to resurrect his Shakespearean insults to raise the tone: 'Damn your eyes, referee!' At half-time, there's a straw poll on whether Nigel should eat his lucky banana. Times are desperate and we vote unanimously for eating.

One thing this side does have is a degree of resilience. The

Hammers step it up in the second half and Bowen goes close with a typical cut inside onto his left foot. The breakthrough comes when Paquetá crosses into the box. Souček heads it back to Bowen, who heads over but a second later is punched in the head by Ryan. It's a clear penalty and a booking for the keeper. Benrahma does well to keep cool while Ryan time wastes, and then he calmly strikes it into the corner.

The crowd becomes more positive as 'West Ham are massive!' rings around the stadium. Zouma makes a great run into the box only to be ignored as Kehrer plays in several wayward crosses. The winner comes with fifteen minutes left. Bowen's corner is flicked on by Zouma, Rice gathers it on the left and crosses into the box. Aguerd's header is cleared off the line, but Antonio is on hand to poke home. He runs to the bouncing Bobby Moore Stand. Carolyn later praises Antonio for an old-school joyful celebration rather than the usual choreographed routine.

It's almost three when Benrahma plays a neat give and go with sub Ings, only to fire over. The Hammers see the game out without too much difficulty and now take a slender lead to the Netherlands. The second leg won't be easy.

We head to Stratford among jubilant fans singing 'We're all having a party when Millwall fucked it up!' (They have just fluffed their bid for the play-offs.) We're joined in Ye Olde Black Bull by Nigel's pal Big Sam, who is possibly off to take Leeds down at the weekend.

Over a pint of Brixton Pale Ale, we learn that Agent Nigel is going to Brentford undercover with a young Bees fan hostage beside him on Sunday. He's also set to complete every home game this season. Matt would have the complete set of home games but he had to work on the evening of the FCSB game when the Queen inconveniently died. He's still upset the game wasn't postponed, allowing him to go to the re-arranged tie. Though none of us can compete with super-fan Lisa's four games in a weekend.

We head off to the Elizabeth Line to see lots of police hopefully wasting the time of the Alkmaar fans. So, it's a one-goal lead and a nervous trip to the pub next Thursday as we seek our first trophy in forty-three years.

Sunday's game at Brentford is a difficult one, with the West Ham players distracted by the chance of European glory. The game proves that, as Michael the Whovian succinctly puts it, 'West Ham have two teams – a middling Premiership side and a middling Championship side' to make up our squad. With nine changes from the Alkmaar game, it's clear Moyes is prioritising Thursday's semi-final and hoping Leicester don't win all three of their remaining matches to overtake the Irons.

Brentford take the lead when Aguerd plays a loose ball out of defence and the unmarked Bryan Mbuemo arrives to stroke home. All too easy, and Fabiański should have done better. Despite several warnings of the dangers of the Bees' long throws, their throws eventually pay off with Brentford winning the ball and Wissa heading home the second goal to leave the Hammers two goals down.

Ings has a snap shot well saved by Raya, but Fabiański also has to make a couple of brilliant saves. Agent Nigel is among the Brentford fans and singles out Cornet as poor and Downes as out of his depth, with no service to Ings who is chasing shadows – though he has seen a few nice touches from Lanzini.

Ings has a goal disallowed for a ludicrous VAR decision. Sub Benrahma's cross comes back off a post and the ball hits Mubama. Lanzini gathers and crosses for Ings to score but VAR rules that Mubama has handballed it. He has his arms out to prevent himself running into the post, and the ball seems to hit his shoulder anyway. Another ridiculous VAR decision.

Even without striker Ivan Toney, Brentford could have scored four or five. It's a really poor performance and proof that without the rested Rice, the Irons struggle. Hopefully it will have been worth resting so many players if the team get a result in the Netherlands, though the reserves have failed to put any pressure on the first team with this performance.

So, it's all eyes on Thursday's semi-final second leg. A bizarre BBC news item might be a bad omen. Their story on the new 3D scans of the wreck of the *Titanic* has pictures of the *Titanic* superimposed on to the London Stadium as a way of emphasising the size of the stricken vessel. The wreck of the *Titanic* stretches from one end of the pitch to the other – and has probably crushed a few pitch invaders carrying corner flags in the process.

Thursday comes around with everyone feeling surprisingly nervous. Can a poor season be changed into a great one? It's off to our new lucky pub The Eagle via Maryland station. Fraser's directions prove better than Nigel's shortcut to the Black Lion, though my trip involves an unexpected detour to Forest Gate as the rear train doors don't open at Maryland station due to the short platform. Lisa has hot-footed it from a poetry reading and Fraser is there with Sinead, who is providing Tayto crisps and peanuts plus East London Pale Ale for our table and a personalised glass for Fraser. Michael is AWOL, possibly watching experimental fringe theatre in the suburbs, while Nigel is searching for a pub showing the game in Wolverhampton where he's visiting his friend Adrian. Strangely, we're the only Hammers fans in the pub but we do get a seat.

It's a raucous atmosphere in the Netherlands and the Hammers come under early pressure. But Zouma and Aguerd have good games at the back, and the side looks determined to learn from last season's semi-final defeat. Antonio starts to use his strength effectively and finds Paquetá, who curls a left foot shot against the outside of the post. It's goalless at the break, though the worrying fact is that Alkmaar are unbeaten in twenty-five matches at home in Europe.

The second half sees more Alkmaar pressure. Rice does get in a long-range effort to force a save, but at the other end, Kehrer very nearly scores an own goal, forcing a fine save from Areola with his misjudged back pass. Alkmaar have a strong claim for a penalty turned down after Aguerd tackles man and ball in the box. Then Areola fails to gather a cross cleanly and the ball touches Zouma's hand, though VAR correctly rules that he couldn't get out of the way.

The occasion might be getting to Matt, who harangues Moyes for being negative, Paquetá for poor passing, Kehrer for poor crossing, Benrahma for lack of end product, Souček for being Souček, Bowen for not taking on his man and Areola for flapping at crosses. He even wants to bring Fornals on, though he surely won't provide much of a goal threat. We try to calm Matt's nerves with more East London Pale Ale.

We're updating the TV-less Nigel on WhatsApp, but dishearteningly, he tells us that he has forgotten his lucky banana. West Ham's chance comes and goes when Aguerd fails to connect properly after a goal-mouth melee. Meanwhile, Fraser sagely states that although we're not playing that well, he can't see Alkmaar scoring. The clock ticks on to ninety minutes and there is set to be a further agonising five minutes of added time.

Paquetá takes it into the corner. But still Alkmaar come forward. We're in the ninety-fourth minute when the ball falls to Fornals on the halfway line. Suddenly, Fornals finds his inner Lionel Messi, nicking the ball through the legs of Jordy Clasie and racing towards the Alkmaar goal. He's still on the edge of the box when he shoots firmly into the corner with an exemplary finish. YEEEEEEES! 'Look at Pab's face!' exclaims Lisa, as Fornals climbs with some difficulty on to the hoardings to salute the joyous Hammers fans going absolutely mental. He is standing aloft in front of St George's Cross flags reading 'Railway Tavern Thetford', 'Benfleet' and 'Gilly Joe Ellis'. We never doubted you, son.

'It's lucky we all stayed so positive,' suggests Matt. Fraser looks emotional as Moyes does a dad jig on the touchline, having probably saved his job. Rice celebrates like a man who will surely reject a move to no-hopers Arsenal. And there is dancing in the streets of Wolverhampton as Nigel realises his cup final breakfast in Kew is back on.

The whistle goes seconds later, and unbelievably the Hammers are through to their first European final since 1976. It's then that some AZ Ultras in quilted jackets start to attack the away section. Some of the West Ham players get involved, concerned that their families are in that section. Downes postures like an Essex geezer and a large West Ham fan called Knowlesy holds back the Herberts in quilted jackets. The police move in, and the trouble is soon quelled. The players return to celebrating with the fans.

Moyes is punching the air, retired Noble is on the pitch in tears again, Cressy is emotional when interviewed on the TV and everyone says Pablo is a 'good lad'. Moyesy looks elated when interviewed by the Cole brothers, Carlton and Joe, along with Robin van Persie.

> We're thrilled. It's a huge achievement for West Ham. It's hard enough to get to any final, never mind a European final … He's [Fornals is] a massive team player … If there was anyone I wanted to score tonight, it would've been Pablo Fornals … We've brought in a lot of international players to get better, but we've really struggled this season. We had to go back to what gets you wins, and thankfully we did that … We had to turn up tonight and find a way of winning.

We celebrate with more Pale Ale. It's just a shame that the final is being played at a small stadium and we probably won't get tickets. But after the semi-final of the Europa League last year, it's real progress to be playing Fiorentina in the Conference final and having the chance of qualifying for the Europa League should we win it. Always in doubt! Come on you Irons!

The next morning it still seems unreal. Moyes has been on the verge of the sack all season. But now we're in a final. It still doesn't seem quite right to see the words 'West Ham' and 'final' in the same sentence. It's forty-three years since the Irons last won a trophy. Leicester, Watford, Portsmouth, Cardiff, Stoke, Wigan, Swansea, Bradford City, Crystal Palace, Birmingham and Fulham have all got to finals more recently than the Hammers, until now. All we have to do next is go out to Prague and win it.

It's going to be next to impossible to get tickets as the Eden Stadium only holds 20,000, and West Ham will only get around 4,900 tickets. I only have nineteen points on my season ticket and the club has 50,000-odd season ticket holders. But contacts might help: I send out emails to Big Joe, Mark who runs Philosophy Football, contacts at *The Guardian* and *The Observer*, my old agent, someone whose son works for UEFA and just about anyone who might hear of one going spare. It's not likely that this will work, though in a fit of optimism I do check whether it's possible to get to Prague by train. Flying to the Czech Republic in an age of global heating would be another moral dilemma. But after forty-three years, it might be a case of by any means necessary. Only Manchester City and Manchester United have won trophies this season. Could we be about to join them?

There's something of a party atmosphere for the final home game of the season against Leeds United, with the Hammers almost mathematically safe and in a European final. Leeds, on the other hand, need to win to have a chance of avoiding relegation. They are on their third manager of the season, which suggests firing the boss doesn't always work.

It's off to the Best Meze cafe to meet Matt and Michael, who is sporting an AK Ultra-style black hoodie, though perhaps the AK lads didn't have a signed *Hamilton* logo on the front of theirs. The big news is that Matt and Lisa are going to Prague on a minibreak for the week of the Europa Conference final, even though they don't have tickets. They think it will make for a good holiday, whatever happens.

The Best's chip portions seem to have got even larger, but after a hasty lunch, we're off by 1 p.m. to make yet another unusual kick-off time of 1.30 p.m. on a Sunday. It's a buoyant stadium, with final flag sellers busy outside. Inside, Fraser – who is watching another bête noire in Sam Allardyce – Nigel and his wife Carolyn make up our number.

In his programme notes, Moyes evokes the memory of David Gold and thanks David Sullivan, Karren Brady and the rest of the board for keeping faith in his management: 'As time goes on you understand people better, and I have found our relationship has become stronger, which can only be good for the club going forward. An increased stadium capacity, lots of new young supporters and European football have been real positives for everyone.'

Club captain Rice pens what sounds like a farewell to the club's fans, writing in his column:

> To get to a final for the first time in 47 years, every one of us will be remembered in West Ham's fans hearts and our history. I've had to deal with a lot on and off the pitch, but I just take it with a pinch of salt really and I just try to play my football, try to play with a smile on my face and every time I put on that shirt, I know what it means. If I don't always play my best, I can never let the badge down, so I always give 100 per cent because the fans, like I say every time, it's a Thursday night they've travelled, and some have missed two days of work and I appreciate every single one of you. From me, a big thank you because even though this season's not been the best, you will sing your hearts out every week and we really appreciate it.

Is that the *Titanic*? No, it's Big Sam Allardyce, who is very visible in his white shirt even from the Billy Bonds Stand. The Leeds fans are in good voice, and their desperate side start well. Patrick Bamford gets behind the home defence to cross, only for Rodrigo to miscontrol. Then Harrison has a shot straight at Fabiański. Leeds take the lead from a throw in, Rodrigo scoring with a fine first-time volley. He runs into the arms of Big Sam, which is a brave thing to do.

That goal sparks the Hammers into life. Rice starts to dominate and Paquetá does some party tricks. Bamford going off injured helps. West Ham equalise fifteen minutes after Leeds score. Fornals lofts a lovely ball over the defence for Bowen to run on to. Bowen gets in a good cross, and Rice volleys into the ground and over Joel Robles. Rice runs to the corner flag to celebrate what might be his last goal for the Irons.

Is Declan really going? He's the best young player we've had since Bobby Moore, so in many ways we're grateful to have had him for six seasons. In a short career, Rice's desire to win leagues and play in Champions League football is understandable. There aren't many players who could make it clear they were not going to sign a new contract yet remain so loved.

Rice looked special from his second appearance as a sub during a 4–0 drubbing at Old Trafford – he immediately stroked the ball around with a calm assurance that suggested he felt perfectly at home on such a stage. Rice is now, along with Man City's Rodri, the best defensive midfielder in the Premier League. He does the simple things well and has a great turn of pace when retrieving the ball from seemingly impossible situations. His upright running style looks effortless, and *The Guardian*'s cartoonist David Squires made us laugh when he portrayed him as a centaur, with a human body and the legs of a horse. Rice has added creativity and goals to his games too, such as his long-range efforts against

Southampton and Nottingham Forest and his run from the halfway line to score against Gent.

Had the appointment of Manuel Pellegrini worked out or had West Ham managed to make the top four rather than finish sixth and seventh under Moyes, we might just have got him to sign a new contract. He's too good to be in a side that is struggling against relegation. What's more, Rice seems to have been very well mentored by former captain Mark Noble. He is honest after defeats, smiles a lot and enjoys the game. He comes across as a proper and humble human being – witness the recent video of him hugging the starstruck kid who bursts into tears upon meeting him. So, it's probably no more years, Declan Rice. It's going to be horrible watching him in a different shirt next season.

The game continues. Paquetá makes a surging run to set up Fornals, who shoots wide. Fornals then feeds Emerson, whose effort is smothered by Robles. Leeds have a good chance to take the lead as Zouma is tackled. Harrison races clear and sets up Gnonto for a scuffed shot that earns derision from the Irons fans. That's why they're going down.

At half-time, we're joined by Steve the Cornish postie, who was dancing in the streets of Crantock last Thursday. Gav and Big Sam Jr turn up too, and there's a quick straw poll on whether at 1–1 Nigel should eat his lucky banana. The vote is he should.

The second half begins amid chants of 'West Ham are

massive!' Leeds look a little intimidated as the Hammers step it up. Paquetá has a long-range shot saved, and Robles does brilliantly to tip over Souček's header from a corner. Carolyn hands out some lucky claret and blue sweets purchased from a ferry in Greenland.

On seventy-two minutes, Paquetá feeds Ings who turns well on the edge of the box to play in Bowen, who skilfully finishes across Robles into the corner. There's a long VAR pause before it's ruled that Bowen is onside by a couple of inches.

There's still time for Summerville (has he left the Communards?) to get through and be thwarted by a fine block from Emerson. At the other end, Paquetá wastefully tries to set up Rice when he could score himself, and Ings misses another chance.

The game is settled when from a West Ham corner, Paquetá somehow bamboozles three Leeds defenders to wriggle in from the touchline, then slaloms across the box and sets up sub Lanzini for a tap-in to make it 3–1. A great moment for Lanzini in his final home game. Big Sam looks like he could do with a pint of wine. Surely that was the assist of the season from Paquetá. And Everton and Leicester can't complain about West Ham's effort in this one.

At the final whistle, the Leeds players look resigned to relegation as they forlornly applaud their fans. The West Ham players come on for a lap of honour with their kids, Declan

Rice receives the Hammer of the Year trophy and Moyes comes over to pump his fists in front of his biggest fans, plus a few doubters.

We head to The Eagle, where Matt discovers that Tayto crisps are made in a castle in Ireland. He suggests they must make a packet there. The drinks flow, with Hackney Haze from the fridge followed by the unexpected arrival of a newly cooled bottle of East London Pale Ale. Michael departs for theatrical environs, Carolyn leaves for her bass class in her bid to become the new Roger Glover and Matt and I head to Maryland station. A difficult season is ending on a high. And on forty points, we think West Ham are finally safe.

The final game of the league season on Survival Sunday is an away game at Leicester. It's West Ham's fifty-sixth match in all competitions. It's a dead rubber for West Ham, and the players aren't going to want to get injured before the Europa Conference League final. Leicester need to win in case Everton fail to beat Bournemouth. Moyes picks a strong side, resting only Souček, Bowen and Zouma.

In the first thirty minutes, several attacks fizzle out and West Ham might do more. Kelechi Iheanacho clips the top of the bar after cutting inside, but Leicester look nervous. A rare moment of quality sees the Foxes take the lead as Barnes plays a swift one-two with Iheanacho, getting beyond Coufal and Downes to angle the ball home.

The Hammers play with more passion after the break.

Jonny Evans heads a corner past his own post and Benrahma curls a fine effort against the base of Leicester's post. Just how many times has Beni hit the post this season? Faes heads home the second goal from a free kick, somehow getting in between West Ham's central defenders. But by then news has come through from Goodison Park that Everton have scored, and the West Ham fans taunt the home crowd with chants of 'Say hello to Millwall!'

Sub Bowen has a shot parried by Daniel Iversen and then lays the rebound into the path of fellow sub Ings, who somehow blazes over. The Irons do pull one back when Ings releases Fornals on the left and he scores with a precise shot in, off the near post. There's still time for a blond Cornet to come on – perhaps it's a disguise in the hope that Matt doesn't recognise him and give him a hard time. He's soon getting in the way of his own player and then kicking his man instead of the ball, which rather sums up his season.

There's not too much to learn from this, apart from the fact it's kept most of the side match fit for Prague. Relegation is a sad comedown for Leicester after their title win in 2016 but as the Hammers fans know, no side is ever too good to go down. It's been a long, bizarre season, cut in half by the World Cup. One more game to go now – and it's a big one.

11

FORTY-THREE YEARS OF HURT

JUNE 2023

In the days leading up to 7 June, there's time to reflect on the enormity of the occasion. To some, the Europa Conference League is a tinpot trophy, but we'll take it if we can win it. West Ham are in their first European final for forty-seven years. Back in 1976, I was a sixteen-year-old on a rainy night at Upton Park watching the Irons beat Eintracht Frankfurt 3–1 in the second leg of the semis to reach the European Cup Winners' Cup final. For the winning goal, Trevor Brooking threw a dummy that sent a defender halfway down the Barking Road. We lost the final 4–2 to Anderlecht but it didn't matter too much. I saw West Ham win the FA Cup at Wembley in 1975 and again in 1980. The Hammers reached the League Cup final in 1981, losing to Liverpool. Surely, finals would come round every few years? But then came the forty-three years of hurt since we last won a trophy.

Sport shouldn't matter that much. But it's been around a long time. Homer wrote some great descriptions of boxing and athletics at the funeral games in *The Iliad*; rival fans supported different teams at Roman chariot races. Simon Barnes in his book *The Meaning of Sport* describes sport as a metaphor, a series of cod battles. He likens sporting drama to Greek mythology; football brings heroes and tales of failure and redemption condensed into a decade or so rather than a whole human lifetime. It appeals to something deep within the human psyche.

I've learned more about life from 6–0 away debacles than easy home wins, which, being a West Ham fan, is just as well. It would have been much easier to support the great Liverpool side in the 1980s, or Manchester United under Sir Alex Ferguson when they won seemingly everything, or Manchester City in the Abu Dhabi-funded Pep Guardiola era. Yet, most teams are, frankly, a bit rubbish. Only two, three or maybe four English teams at the most win a trophy each season. Numerous big city clubs flounder around without too much sign of progress. Perhaps it is the rarity of any kind of success that keeps football fans coming back. A trophy after years of adversity means more than easy triumphs. Perhaps football is about exchanging years of frustration for one day of utter wonder.

Every supporter believes their team has a monopoly on misery. But like Roy Batty in *Blade Runner*, I've seen things you people wouldn't believe. West Ham had their best ever finish of third in the league in 1986 but didn't get into Europe because of the ban following the Heysel Stadium disaster. With Frank McAvennie and Tony Cottee scoring at will, for a long time I really thought we might win our first title.

But a decline set in. West Ham were relegated in 1989, and John Lyall was sacked and replaced by Lou Macari, who only lasted seven months. While in the Second Division under Macari, the Irons managed to lose a 1989 League Cup semi-final at Oldham 6–0. And that was only the first leg. The Hammers returned to the big time under Billy Bonds and duly went down again. They bounced back to the Premier League boosted by new gaffer Harry Redknapp's *Minder*-esque transfer dealings and some maverick genius from Paolo Di Canio. We finished fifth under Redknapp in 1999 but still won no trophies.

The enjoyable madness of the Redknapp era was summed up by Di Canio asking to be substituted, wrestling with Frank Lampard for the ball to take a penalty and then inspiring a 5–4 win against Bradford City after being 4–2 down.

In 1999, the Hammers did win a sort of trophy, the UEFA Intertoto Cup, which was really a pre-season qualifying round to get into the UEFA Cup. The Hammers beat Jokerit and Heerenveen before the season started and then played

Metz in the finals. No one really considered it a trophy though – apart from Fraser, who was in Metz on 24 August for the 3–1 second-leg win and says he was 'braving a malicious water-cannon-toting French steward and menacing riot police'. It was an achievement to get into the UEFA Cup, of course, but West Ham were eliminated pretty quickly, beaten by Steaua Bucureşti in round two.

West Ham also became a pub quiz question. Which team won and lost the same League Cup semi-final in different millenniums? At the back end of 1999, West Ham beat Aston Villa on penalties in a League Cup quarter-final. Substitute Manny Omoyinmi came on for the final minutes. However, Manny had already played in an earlier round for Gillingham while on loan and was in fact ineligible. No one at the club seemed to have checked. The league ordered the tie to be replayed, and in 2000, West Ham inevitably lost to Villa. It was all so very West Ham.

It was also typical to blow the record £18 million transfer fee received from Leeds for Rio Ferdinand. Redknapp spent the dosh on the likes of Titi Camara, Rigobert Song, Raggy Soma and Svetoslav Todorov, none of whom became Hammers legends. We were getting used to scattergun signings. Though the Hammers did sign Christian Dailly, who had curly hair and his own risqué fans' song. Christian became the love of many Hammers' lives.

In Glenn Roeder's second season as boss, the Irons managed

to not win at home until late January and then achieved the considerable feat of going down with a record forty-two points in 2003. In that period, the Hammers ended up selling most of the England side, having unloaded some brilliant talent in Rio Ferdinand, Frank Lampard, Joe Cole, Michael Carrick, Glen Johnson and Jermain Defoe. Had that side stayed together, then anything might have been possible.

New gaffer Alan Pardew achieved promotion at the second attempt after winning the Championship play-off final against Preston North End. He then took the Irons to the 2006 FA Cup final after Marlon Harewood scored the semi-final winner against Middlesbrough at Villa Park. The cup final was the moment our trophy drought was set to end, with the lads 3–2 up after ninety minutes at the Millennium Stadium in Cardiff. That was until Lionel Scaloni (whatever happened to him?) hoofed a clearance towards the Liverpool midfield rather than putting the ball into touch. The ball reached one Steven Gerrard, who dispatched a hypersonic missile into Shaka Hislop's net. Nigel Reo-Coker headed against the post in extra time and West Ham lost the greatest final of modern times on penalties because the big clubs always seem to win shoot-outs.

The club was bought by Icelandic millionaire Björgólfur Guðmundsson, aided by biscuit baron chairman Eggert Magnússon. We signed Carlos Tevez and Javier Mascherano but forgot that they were owned by a third party. For a long time, the gaffer favoured Harewood and Hayden Mullins over the Argentine superstars. Pardew went and was replaced by Alan Curbishley. West Ham looked certain to be relegated the season after reaching the FA Cup final, but this being West Ham, Curbishley mastered the 'great escape' as the Irons won seven of their final nine matches, ending with a 1–0 win at Man United, the goal being scored by Tevez. West Ham escaped with a fine over the Tevez transfer, much to the annoyance of relegated Sheffield United.

West Ham's owner Guðmundsson then lost all his dosh in the 2008 financial crisis. It was all going a bit *Wizard of Oz.* Curbishley left as players were sold and was replaced by Gianfranco Zola. Memorably, the club lost its shirt sponsor, XL, and the team had to turn out with blank patches hastily sewn across their shirts.

West Ham almost went down again but were saved financially by new owners David Sullivan and David Gold, who sacked Zola and appointed Avram Grant, who had just reached a Champions League final with Chelsea. Grant never looked comfortable in the job. At Wigan, we went 2–0 up and then lost 3–2 to confirm relegation, all rounded off by a plane flying overhead carrying a banner reading, 'Avram Grant: Millwall Legend.'

Big Sam Allardyce was the necessary shock medicine. He won the 2012 Championship play-off final against Blackpool and established the Hammers back in the Premier League.

In 2014, the Hammers lost a League Cup semi-final to Manchester City 9–0 on aggregate, having lost the first leg at the Etihad 6–0. Big Sam kept the team stable but struggled to win over the fans, most notably cupping his ear to the crowd after boos greeted a 2–1 win against the ten men of Hull City, and his contract was not renewed.

Slaven Bilić was the right manager to celebrate the final season at the Boleyn Ground, the 2015–16 season. Dimitri Payet was brilliant. West Ham looked set to get to the FA Cup final but lost at home to Man United in the quarter-final, having drawn at Old Trafford. The Irons managed to drop to seventh place on the final day after being in the top six all season.

The move to the London Stadium brought a new level of misery to fans who missed Upton Park. The distance from the pitch was a problem, as was the green carpet over the athletics track. Fans who wanted to stand found themselves next to others who wanted to sit. Payet became homesick and the 'We've got Payet!' song became something much more expletive-ridden as he left to return to France. West Ham made the Europa League but somehow managed to find a Romanian bogey side, losing in successive seasons to FC Astra Giurgiu. Bilić's side struggled on the wide-open spaces surrounded by green plastic, and after a 4–1 home defeat to Liverpool, Slaven was fired.

During Moyes's first spell at the club, a 3–0 home defeat

to Burnley was interrupted by pitch invaders. Fans unhappy with the state of the club and the stadium move tried to storm the boardroom. Mark Noble even had to act as an impromptu bouncer, carrying one invader off the pitch.

Manuel Pellegrini was meant to take West Ham to the next level. His side finished tenth in his first season, but his reign ended with the side in relegation trouble the following season. Many of his signings underperformed, including the hapless goalkeeper Roberto, the injury-ravaged Jack Wilshere, Andriy Yarmolenko, Sébastien Haller, Lucas Pérez and Carlos Sánchez. We knew things were turning a bit surreal at Christmas when Michail Antonio skidded on ice and crashed his car while dressed as a snowman.

Back came Moyes to sign Bowen and Souček, convert Antonio into a striker and save West Ham again in the second half of 2019–20. Lockdown arrived. And then something changed. Playing behind closed doors, West Ham finished sixth. Moyes did his dad dance when Lanzini scored at Spurs, Rice was a colossus, Bowen was on fire and dating Dani Dyer and the Irons were back in the Europa League. The stands behind the goals at the London Stadium were squared off and it started to feel more like a football ground.

Then came the run to the semi-final of the Europa League where we lost to Eintracht Frankfurt in a very West Ham way, conceding a goal in the first minute of the home leg and having Cresswell sent off early in the away leg. We've struggled this season but have somehow, gloriously, reached a European final. But defeat could mean it's all forgotten and still result in the sacking of Moyes. Yet, a victory could make Moyes the club's most successful manager since Ron Greenwood and John Lyall. It really is an all-or-nothing game.

Since West Ham last won something, I've rented in twelve different houses, become a journalist, published books, got married, had two children, bought a house and climbed all 214 Wainwright fells in the Lake District. Punk, new romantic, acid house, grunge and Oasis versus Blur have all been and gone. We've had nine Prime Ministers in that time.

For those of us who have travelled from 1980 to 2023, from young men to old codgers, it's been a long journey. Is it possible that Declan Rice can become the first Hammers captain since Moore and Bonds to lift a trophy? Or are the Irons going to make me wait another forty-three years? Just this once, let's hope fortune is not always hiding.

12

THE MIRACLE OF PRAGUE

JUNE 2023

Suddenly, there's a tickle. Big Joe is on my mobile saying that my old pal Denis might have a spare ticket for Prague. Denis phones me up at 11 p.m. on Monday night. His pal in UEFA has come up with a pair of tickets. Of course I'd like to go! I check with Nicola that she can look after our dog Vulcan, and it's sorted.

I've known Denis since the late 1980s, when we both wrote for the West Ham fanzine *Fortune's Always Hiding*. We bonded at our first game watching Jimmy 'The Tree' Quinn score against Brighton in the old Second Division, back in the days when we used to beat the Seagulls. We co-wrote the book *The Lad Done Bad* together, along with Andrew Shields. For a long time, Denis sat with our group in the East Stand at Upton Park and is now a season ticket holder in the West Stand at the London Stadium.

Denis is from Northern Ireland but adopted the Hammers when working in London for *NME* and *Time Out*. He's now at *The Guardian* and never forgets a contact, hence his man at UEFA who has come up with the goods.

Denis's super-efficient wife Clare is on her laptop and busy booking a flight to Munich and a train from Munich to Prague as we speak. I scan my passport and email it over to her. I've only flown once in the previous twelve years in a bid to reduce my carbon output and lessen global warming, so this means something of a compromise of my eco principles. But I hope that in the great climate change reckoning, this will be seen as exceptional circumstances. West Ham fans haven't troubled anyone's carbon footprint much in forty-three years.

By 12.30 a.m., travel arrangements are sorted and I'm feeling giddy with excitement. How brilliant of Denis to include me as his companion. The only proviso is that we have to wear suits, as we're in with the prawn sandwich set, but this is a case of by any means necessary. Somehow, Denis has managed to convince the UEFA team that I am a celebrated West Ham author and blogger.

Over the next couple of days, I research and book a twin hotel room close to Munich station, where we are overnighting before catching the train. Next, I find a boutique hotel in Prague that costs £140 a night, which is fairly reasonable considering most places are charging £200 or more.

Then I have to tell my West Ham season ticket-holding pals on WhatsApp that I have found a ticket, feeling a little guilty that they are missing out. Everyone is decent and congratulates me, though they must be envious. Of course, I'd rather be with the real fans than sitting with the suits, but it's better to see the final with them than not at all.

The thirteen-day wait before we travel is what the 'phoney war' in 1939 must have felt like. At least my passport is up to date. The day of travel begins with a feeling of both trepidation and excitement. If nothing else, Prague is a beautiful city for sightseeing, even if we do mess it up on the pitch. Having first seen West Ham in 1970, I'm finally attending my first European away fixture. Not that we've been in Europe much.

Sadly, there will be no cup final breakfast in Nigel's gaff at Kew as we'll be in Prague. After loitering in the lounge at Heathrow, Denis and I are soon on the flight to Munich. Then it's a short journey to Munich where we are staying in the Mercure Hotel near the main station. The area is slightly sleazy, full of hotels and table-dancing joints, but we find a noodle bar and enjoy a late dinner before retiring.

In the morning, we hastily buy baguettes for the five-hour train journey to Prague. We sit in an old-fashioned six-person compartment and enjoy a better way of seeing the country. Denis wonders why Moyes can't make more use of a talented squad in between attending to emails on his laptop. We head into the green countryside of the Czech Republic, and a woman comes on board with a trolley, serving communist-era coffee, instant and without milk.

In that day's *Evening Standard*, Ken Dyer interviews David Moyes, who reveals that the 'Moyes Out' banner at Fulham hurt but he is building something at West Ham and wants to stay:

> I know football is about the here and now, and you can't look back, but it did hurt and it was disappointing. The fact is I had been asked twice to come and help keep the club in the Premier League and this season we had to do it again. In between that though, I hope everyone had enjoyed a great couple of seasons … When I saw that banner it was hurtful because it drains your power and strength to do things. When people continually question you though, it drains you. I've got to say it wasn't a good time. Did I feel lonely? Hugely. Management is a lonely business.

In *The Times*, Jonathan Northcroft has written a piece headlined, 'David Moyes is loyal, humble, giving and stands apart.' Northcroft looks back at the influence of Moyes's father, David Sr, who ran a junior side at the famous Drumchapel Amateurs in Glasgow and the family philosophy of 'don't fuss – get out there and get on with it.'

Northcroft also points out that, despite Moyes being derided for unsuccessful spells at Manchester United, Real Sociedad and Sunderland, Moyes took Preston to a Championship play-off final, had nine top eight finishes with Everton, was thirty minutes from a Champions League semi-final with Man United, twice saved West Ham from relegation, reached sixth and seventh with the Hammers and got to a Europa League semi-final.

The piece concludes:

> He stands out among football people I've met. For his loyalty, his humility and the time he gives to others. In lockdown he delivered fruit and veg to the elderly and it took months for the story to be reported because he didn't want anyone to know about it. 'Don't fuss – get out there and get on with it' was his take. If he lifts the cup, no triumph would be more authentic, born of more grit, more deserved.

Matt and Lisa, already in Prague, report on WhatsApp that in the Old Town Square the famous astronomical chiming clock is being regaled with chants of 'You've only got one song!' Lisa also says it's worth seeing the stunning art nouveau architecture of the upper section of Praha station – as West Ham fans like a bit of art nouveau. Matt and Lisa have, of course, already been to the most important game of the week in Prague, a 0–0 relegation play-off second leg between Pardubice and Viagem Příbram (formerly Dukla Prague, whose away kit, as immortalised in the song by Half Man Half Biscuit, is sometimes worn by Matt to Hammers' matches).

Arriving in Prague, we discover that our hotels are pleasingly close to the station. We take a selfie making crossed arm Hammers salutes outside Praha station. Denis is in a more upmarket hotel than mine but handily, it's just around the corner. My cheaper room is still impressive with its coffee maker and fridge. We dump our stuff, shower and head out. Replica Hammers shirts seem to be everywhere. There's a giant replica of the Europa Conference League trophy in a nearby square where people are taking selfies with West Ham flags.

We stroll through the lovely architecture of the Old Town to meet Matt and Lisa plus fellow Hammers Danny and daughter Issy at Pizza Nuova. It's a buzz to meet fellow football expatriates in a place that isn't Stratford. Culture buffs Matt and Lisa reason that they will have a great week holidaying in Prague, even if they don't get a ticket.

Denis has shared a press release from Reuters on the estimated 20,000 West Ham fans arriving in Prague, motto 'no ticket no problem'. Frank Haughton, the owner of several Irish pubs in Prague, is quoted saying:

> When football comes sometimes you get a bit nervous about what kind of supporter you're going to get – but these guys

> started arriving yesterday and I must say so far they're a very nice crew. These guys mainly drink beer. We expect our sales to be 95 per cent alcohol and 5 per cent food.

As much as 5 per cent? We've probably had most of the West Ham fans' food allowance at our meal. After our huge and enjoyable pizzas plus some Czech beer we head back to our hotels.

Though we don't meet him, comedian Phil Whelans from the podcast *Stop! Hammer Time* is in town, after a 6.30 a.m. flight from London. His sometimes podcast guest Mark Gower is there too and likens the influx of claret and blue to the mods arriving in Brighton in the film *Quadrophenia*. 'And it was like Ian Bishop was the Face – he was on my flight!' adds Mark. Mark has travelled on a 4.30 a.m. flight from Heathrow to Frankfurt, then a connecting flight to Vienna and a five-hour train ride from Vienna to Prague. He's staying in a 34-person dorm at the Czech Inn hostel, which is meant to be for eighteen- to 39-year-olds. Mark is fifty-one.

Don Perretta, my old *Fortune's Always Hiding* co-contributor, is somewhere in Prague. So is Jacqui Hughes, a red-haired super fan and coordinator of the Upton Parklife Facebook group. As a girl, she once ruffled Bobby Moore's hair as he came out of the players' tunnel at Upton Park. Supporters seem to be arriving by infinite routes and combinations of flights, trains and cars. They really are following West Ham over land and sea.

The next day we have a hectic sightseeing schedule to complete, let alone a game of football to watch. It starts off with meeting Matt and Lisa at the Castle (an area of historic buildings immortalised by Kafka, not a pub). After overshooting on the bus, we eventually climb up the picturesque Golden Lane to view Lobkowicz Palace, the St Vitus Cathedral, the Old Royal Palace and numerous other epic buildings atop the hill. There's a superb aerial view of the city from here, and fans from both sides are milling around. Denis approaches a group of friendly purple-shirted Fiorentina fans. One of them who speaks good English says he also likes the Hammers in England. Bizarrely, he pulls up his shirt to reveal a 'fortune's always hiding' tattoo on his torso. We pose for a photo, and it all seems very good-natured so far.

We then walk back down the hill to the famous Charles Bridge, full of stone statues of great Czech figures from the past. Indeed, one statue seems to have a supplicant West Ham fan praying behind bars. Lisa has been reading her guidebooks and gets us all to rub the foot of the St John of Nepomuk statue, as this gesture brings good luck. Perhaps the Queen Elizabeth II Bridge over the Thames at Grays will be filled with similar statues of West Ham's players should we win tonight.

We move on through the Old Town Square, which is full

of West Ham geezers drinking beer in the sunshine. In one tourist shop, two tickets for the final are on sale at 1,000 euros each. Then it's on to lunch at Pizza Nuova again with Denis's gang of Danny, Issy, Tony and Phil plus Matt and Lisa, followed by a wander around the art deco splendour of the Municipal House restaurant.

In the afternoon, a concerned message arrives from my daughter Lola saying, 'Stay safe out there, Dad!' A breaking news item reports, 'Dozens arrested after West Ham fans were attacked before tonight's Europa Conference final in Prague.' It's a bit worrying my family don't think a 63-year-old man could see off a few Ultras. A group of Italian Herberts have set off smoke bombs and attacked a bar full of West Ham fans in the Old Town. But it seems the police have moved in quickly and arrests have been made. 'Dad's hanging with the bigwigs not the Ultras!' concludes Lola. Thankfully, there isn't any further trouble.

After lunch, we walk back to the hotel to pick up the passes for the match, which we place in the safe in Denis's room. We don't have time to fit in the Kafka Museum – frankly supporting West Ham is Kafkaesque enough. Then it's a trip by taxi to the Saints Cyril and Methodius Cathedral with Denis, Matt and Lisa. We enter the museum in the crypt dedicated to the memory of the seven commandos who died after assassinating Nazi Reinhard Heydrich, one of the principal architects of the Final Solution, in 1942. The commandos were besieged in the crypt but spent a long time heroically fighting off their Nazi occupiers before killing themselves with cyanide pills. Well, that puts football in perspective. Denis is so interested in the museum that I'm a bit worried he might forget about the game.

We walk back to our hotels for a swift shower and to change into our suits. At least I have a claret West Ham tie and a blue shirt to show my allegiance. As we wait for the UEFA bus to the Eden Arena, we bump into two West Ham fans who turn out to be Jack Collison's uncles. Collison could have been a great player for West Ham but his career was sadly ended by a serious knee injury.

As we travel slowly towards the ground, the streets are packed with fans heading towards the stadium. A ring of police keeps those without tickets away from the immediate vicinity.

We head into the stand at the Eden Arena and use our lanyards to buzz in. We enjoy the corporate hospitality, as Denis spots James Corden and our pal Big Joe who is going to Australia the next day – as you do. The pre-match entertainment would certainly satisfy my fellow season ticket-holder Nigel, as it's a load of middle-aged blokes playing air guitar to AC/DC, Nirvana and other guitar giants. We take a besuited selfie. It's hard to believe that after all the miles of travelling we're actually here.

Wearing our suits and green lanyards and trying to look

like UEFA technocrats, we saunter around the VIP area. We have absolutely scored on the seats, which are right above the halfway line. Obviously, we'd rather be in among the real fans, but it has to be said that the Thai curry on offer is rather good, even if the only beer is Heineken. Across the room we can see Karren Brady and David Sullivan having their pre-match repast. It's all a bit different to my 1980 experience of a beery concourse full of light ale and lager. Though a couple of VIPs are in old-style replica West Ham shirts with Bobby Moore's number six on the back, having obviously also called in some favours.

On WhatsApp, Alison and her son Scott – who have sat behind us in the Billy Bonds Stand since the stadium move but this season gave up their tickets mainly to look after Alison's elderly mum Val – send a picture of themselves looking nervous on their sofa in Clacton. Plus, a picture of Alison's sister Roz at the Essex University bar wearing a West Ham T-shirt and claret and blue trousers. Another old school friend, Mark, says he is watching in the Argyle Bar in Edinburgh.

A photo arrives from the 'Eaglezone' in Leyton where Fraser, Michael, Nigel, Carolyn and Big Sam are gathered. Luckily for Moyes and his men, Nigel is brandishing his lucky banana and its kinetic energy is surely zooming across the continent towards Prague.

Matt and Lisa have entered the fan zone at Letna Park

where some 20,000 ticketless Hammers fans have gathered. It's a sweltering day and they struggle to find water, being perhaps the only West Ham fans after something that isn't lager or a kebab. Eventually, a security guard finds them some. There are six big screens and the biggest one next to the stage is totally rammed. Getting served at the bar is rather like the old Central pub in Upton Park on a bad day. They choose a quieter screen further out, dragging wooden benches over from a tent-like structure in the middle of the park. They've missed Chesney Hawkes's set and are now being regaled with pre-match techno and house music. Another friend from Islington, Pip, is also in the fan zone, and reports that two of his friends have acquired match tickets for a whopping £2,000 each.

I take my seat for a moment. It's an hour before kick-off, but the ground is full. It's a small stadium with a cracking atmosphere as the West Ham fans sing 'West Ham are massive! Everywhere we go!' It's disappointing to see some empty seats in the Fiorentina end, though the Viola fans do make a splendid racket with their drums and chants. This final means something to both sets of fans, though West Ham fans have certainly colonised around two thirds of the stadium. Never underestimate someone from Essex in search of a ticket.

Moyes has made two big calls, bringing in Emerson at left-back in place of Cresswell and preferring Vladimír 'Robo-Cop' Coufal to Kehrer at right-back. It's tough on Cresswell, who has been at the club ten years. Fiorentina have sprung a surprise by omitting the competition's top scorer, Arthur Cabral.

It's knotted stomach time as the teams take to the pitch amid a sea of claret and purple flags. Giant club badges adorn the pitch. A huge chorus of 'Bubbles' goes up as the teams stand with their young mascots. The noise sounds more like 100,000 people than the official attendance of 17,363. Fiorentina are in their traditional purple, while West Ham play in their away strip of white shirts with an orange flash.

Rice and Cristiano Biraghi shake hands and exchange pendants. Spanish referee Carlos del Cerro Grande places the ball on the centre spot and Fiorentina kick off. Antonio gets a fairly tame shot in at the Fiorentina goal in the first minute to slightly ease the West Ham nerves. A minute later, Biraghi rolls around on the grass after an innocuous challenge from Bowen. Has the Grealish Sniper travelled to Prague? Manager Vincenzo Italiano leaps around his technical area like a very irate pedestrian who has just seen a mugger run off with his top-of-the-range iPhone.

Rice makes a fine and fair tackle in the box, which causes Nicolás González to go down holding his face. It seems there's a plan to wind up the West Ham players and perhaps intimidate the referee into giving free kicks. A few plastic glasses are thrown from the West Ham end at González, and you can feel the West Ham fans getting agitated.

Rolando Mandragora fires well wide in a cagey opening spell. Benrahma goes up for an aerial challenge with Dodô and his arm catches the Fiorentina man, who goes down with a bloodied nose. It's an accidental clash but is likely to enflame the already febrile atmosphere.

After twelve minutes, Rice volleys just wide after a defender half-clears Coufal's long throw. The next player to go down is Christian Kouamé after feeling an arm on his back from Coufal. 'West Ham are massive! Everywhere we go!' chant the Irons fans. Jović is blocked from shooting by Aguerd. But after twenty minutes, it's clear most of the passing is coming from Fiorentina with West Ham only enjoying 30 per cent of possession.

Sofyan Amrabat is dominating midfield, and Fiorentina are hustling for every ball. This is attritional stuff. Still, finals are seldom great games, and the thought occurs that when the players tire someone like Paquetá might eventually get to show a bit of class.

There are ironic cheers from the Hammers fans when Antonio, who is getting some rough treatment, finally wins a free kick. But West Ham are struggling to keep hold of the ball and you wonder if a long season and the big occasion are getting to the players. Fiorentina win a corner and again plastic glasses fly on to the pitch as it's taken. It's starting to turn ugly, and a 9 p.m. local time kick-off now seems particularly unwise, allowing the fans to spend all day drinking in sun-drenched Prague.

Benrahma is booked for diving on the edge of the box, which is a sign that West Ham are struggling. The referee has got it right though the West Ham fans don't agree, chanting 'You're not fit to referee!'

A great run from González is stopped by Aguerd at the price of a corner. Again, some idiots throw plastic cups at the taker, Biraghi, who goes down with blood streaming from a neck wound. The referee picks up the vape that has hit him. There is no excuse for this, and I hope that whoever threw it gets a lifetime ban. Biraghi is fitted with a purple bandage around his head. We really don't want this to be the enduring image of the final.

The West Ham players, with Rice and Zouma taking the initiative, head into the corner to appeal to their own fans to stop throwing objects. UEFA protocols kick in as the referee stops the game and an announcement goes out on the PA and big screen asking the fans to stop throwing objects.

After a four-minute pause, Biraghi's corner is headed clear, and the game becomes a little calmer. Paquetá finally gets on the ball to feed Benrahma, who wins a corner. This is more like it. Emerson's first corner is headed away and his second results in a blocked shot from Rice. Emerson then surges forward to win a free kick, which is again headed away. At least the Irons have applied a little bit of pressure, while for all Fiorentina's possession, they have yet to get a shot on target.

But then the four minutes of added time almost ends in disaster. González whips in a cross, Areola tips Kouamé's header on to the post and Jović heads the rebound home. Mercifully, VAR intervenes and correctly rules that Jović scored from an offside position. Still, that's a warning.

Denis and I retreat into the corporate scoffing area to reflect on a tough first half. Michael my Whovian pal sends a WhatsApp message noting that the Fiorentina team contains both Dodo, who was once William Hartnell's companion, and Mandragora, as in the *Doctor Who* story 'The Masque of Mandragora'. If we can win, it might mark the regeneration of West Ham. Though it's going to take more than the Doctor reversing the polarity of the neutron flow to win this one I reflect, taking a corporate bottle of Heineken to try and ease my worries.

Fiorentina bring on top scorer Cabral for the second half while the Hammers remain unchanged. The side start with new intensity as Rice pumps the ball into the box and Bowen goes down, hoping for a penalty. Benrahma wins a corner, resulting in a booming chant of 'Come on you Irons!' before it's cleared. Aguerd is unlucky to be booked after an aerial clash of heads and Kouamé has Fiorentina's first shot on target.

The breakthrough arrives on fifty-seven minutes. Paquetá wins a throw-in. Coufal puts a long throw into the box and

Bowen challenges Biraghi for the loose ball. A great shout of 'handball!' goes up from the West Ham fans and Bowen runs to the ref frantically tapping his arm.

The appeal goes to VAR and the referee heads to the monitor. The referee is surrounded by Fiorentina players as he looks at the screen but gives the penalty. Benrahma has to wait an age to take the spot-kick. Meanwhile, Zouma has had to depart with injury and be replaced by Kehrer. But Benrahma has never missed a penalty for West Ham, and displaying great composure, he sends the keeper the wrong way to wallop the ball into the top corner. The bank of West Ham fans in front of him explodes with joy, and he goes to stand on the hoardings by the corner flag, arms aloft above his teammates.

Could this be it at last? One-nil with a dodgy penalty. We'll take that. 'Oh, Saïd Benrahma!' chant the Irons fans to the tune of 'Seven Nation Army' by the White Stripes. And then it's 'West Ham are massive!'

However, Fiorentina are still passing the ball around nicely. They have a penalty appeal turned down when Mandragora's shot hits Kehrer's chest and is deflected on to his hand. But he's shot from point-blank range at Kehrer, and the appeal is correctly waved away.

The Irons' lead only lasts five minutes. Amrabat plays a diagonal ball towards the right wing. Emerson loses a headed duel with González and the ball falls to Giacomo

Bonaventura, who takes a great touch with his left foot and turns sharply to shoot past Areola with his right foot. Now it's the turn of the Fiorentina end to explode with a cauldron of noise. It means just as much to their fans as ours.

Moyes holds his hands to his head. At this point I'm convinced we'll lose, as La Viola look a decent footballing side. With twenty minutes left, Paquetá suddenly shows a glimpse of class, prodding a great little ball through to Antonio who shoots against the legs of Pietro Terracciano. But Antonio had drifted offside, and the flag is up.

Soon, Mandragora is putting a great chance just wide from the edge of the area. Nikola Milenković is booked for a late tackle on Paquetá, who is threatening to break down the left wing. Fornals comes on to replace Benrahma and loses possession with a hasty first touch. Time to calm down.

A long throw from Coufal causes some panic in the box and Součck's shot is saved, though the ref gives a foul as Antonio's backheel has caught Milenković. 'I won't be able to cope with penalties,' I tell Denis. Ten minutes left and we're surely heading towards extra time. The corner comes to nothing.

But this Moyes side has resilience and team spirit. A long free kick from Aguerd sees a towering header from Souček tipped past the post by Terracciano. That was route one, but it almost worked. The corner is cleared to Rice, who plays a poor cross into touch.

There is nothing to separate the sides. The West Ham fans try to urge their side on with 'Come on you Irons!' Igor comes on for Fiorentina. Amrabat is booked for a late tackle on Emerson. There's a nervous moment after eighty-eight minutes when Paquetá loses possession on the edge of his own box and Amrabat fires in a shot that is gathered by the leaping Areola.

One minute left. Coufal plays a free kick into the box but Terracciano is fouled. Half a minute left. The keeper boots the ball into the West Ham half. Aguerd wins a header. Souček, doing a lot of unsung work in midfield, makes a nuisance of himself and in the tussle a loose ball falls to Paquetá. He takes one look and plays an instant through ball to Bowen, who takes a touch and is outpacing Igor. Time appears to stop. Terracciano is advancing; there's an agonising pause before Bowen strikes his shot. The ball brushes the top of the keeper's knee and rolls into the net.

Bowen rushes into the corner with a knee slide. The West Ham end is a mass of arms and bouncing blokes from Benfleet. Moyes is channelling David Pleat with a dash and jig on to the pitch. The subs are on the grass too. The two Italian dignitaries next to us walk out in disgust, not knowing that West Ham are quite capable of blowing a lead. Italiano leaps up and down like a man being attacked by hornets. There's a VAR check but Bowen is definitely onside.

There are five minutes of added time. I'm gripped by abject

terror. 'West Ham are massive!' echoes around the stadium. Ogbonna comes on for Antonio to try and bolster the defence. Fiorentina pump balls into the box. The ghost of Steven Gerrard is surely out there somewhere and wearing a purple shirt – we never hold on to leads. Fornals hoofs it clear of the box. The five minutes is up, but still we play on.

In the sixth minute of added time, Paquetá wins a free kick to huge cheers. Nearly eight minutes of added time has gone. It's a free kick to Fiorentina on the right. Their keeper is coming up. Areola comes out for a final cross, misses and the ball drifts out for a goal kick. And then comes the final whistle after ninety-eight minutes. Blimey.

Forty-three years of hurt is over. Moyes is on the pitch as an army of subs and staff race for the far corner of the stadium. No one can quite believe it. It's not been a great game, we haven't played well, but somehow, we've done it. On the BT Sport coverage, commentator Adam Summerton is hollering, 'History makers! Legends! The wait is finally over! Bowen's goal is enough. Moyes has made it happen!'

We've won a trophy! WE'VE WON A TROPHY! It's fifty-eight years since the Hammers last won a European trophy, the European Cup Winners' Cup at Wembley in 1965, and forty-three years since we won the FA Cup. And now as winners we're in the Europa League, something we'd normally only achieve through finishing in the top six. For the first time in the club's history, West Ham will be in Europe for three successive seasons.

Jarrod Bowen stops to simply look at the crowd and take it all in. Rarely can his love life have been celebrated with such abandon. A massive chorus breaks out of 'JARROD BOWEN'S ON FIRE / AND HE'S SHAGGING DANI DYER!' The players are pumping their arms up and down in unison, despite the lyrics not being quite suitable for primetime viewing. Even Moyes is joining in, apparently now freed from desire.

What a moment for the club and for sixty-year-old Moyesy. He's been unfairly derided all his career for not winning anything apart from the League One title with Preston, though he did reach an FA Cup final with Everton. At Brighton, the Irons fans said he didn't know what he was doing. But maybe he did. Now, after his 1,097th game as a manager, Moyes is a trophy winner and is pumping his fists into the night air. 'Go on Moyesy!' shouts overexcited summariser Robbie Savage on the BT Sport coverage.

In these days of corporate football, the big clubs seem to regard winning trophies as routine. But the outpouring of emotion here is a refreshing antidote, and the celebrations last forever. Rice is being carried on the shoulders of Ogbonna and celebrating like a man who surely can't join a small club from Highbury. Mark Noble is on the pitch in tears, the backroom staff are all there, as are James Collins, Carlton Cole and Joe Cole. Moyes is with his 87-year-old dad. 'WE KNOW WHAT WE ARE / CHAMPIONS OF EUROPE / WE KNOW WHAT WE ARE!' sings a heaving mass of claret and blue.

No one under fifty in the crowd has ever seen West Ham win a major trophy. Some people are celebrating wildly; other fans are holding their hands to their faces in utter disbelief. The cameras pan to a bloke in a trilby taking photos in the crowd – it's my old pal Steve 'North Bank Norman' Rapport who founded the *Fortune's Always Hiding* fanzine and has somehow found a ticket and made it to the game from his home in New Orleans.

In the Prague fan zone, it has taken Matt and Lisa ages to celebrate Bowen's goal as the screens keep showing and re-showing the offside lines. After that, everyone is just pacing around as the five added minutes stretch to eight. Many fans seem utterly dazed and confused at the final whistle, unable to believe a European trophy has been won, before everyone starts leaping around and hugging strangers in a flurry of flying beer, shirtless blokes, bubbles and claret and blue tickertape.

The last time West Ham won something, 'Geno' by Dexys Midnight Runners was at number one in the charts and Margaret Thatcher was Prime Minister. There were no mobile phones or home computers, and VHS video was cutting-edge technology.

A heartfelt 'One more year, one more year, Declan Rice!' goes up. Benrahma and Fornals get their own chants. Rice runs to his brothers in the crowd and dances with his young nephew Jackson on his shoulders. Denis notices minority shareholder Daniel Křetínský come up to offer congratulations to Karren Brady, who has been dancing away to 'Freed From Desire'.

And on the pitch is a green victory arch with 'West Ham' and 'Winners' on it, two words that are not commonly associated. Moyes comes up first to receive his medal, getting a hug and word in his ear from chairman David Sullivan who is wearing a claret blazer. Now it's the turn of the players to walk past the trophy and kiss it. Finally, Rice steps up to hold the trophy and rank with Moore and Bonds in West Ham history. He moves to the front of the team huddle and lifts the trophy to a hail of glitter and a massive roar. The PA plays Queen's 'We Are the Champions'. Then it's 'I'm Forever Blowing Bubbles' and a dash to the fans followed by Neil Diamond's 'Sweet Caroline'.

A lot of solid professionals are finally getting rewarded with medals, like long-standing servants Ogbonna and Antonio, who has carried our attack for four seasons. There's the non-playing subs too, like the experienced Aaron Cresswell, who must have been gutted to be left out, and Manuel Lanzini. And what a moment for kids like Mubama and Potts, who were both on the bench. At the other end of the scale, Emerson has now won all three European trophies: the Champions League and Europa League with Chelsea and the much-superior Europa Conference League with West Ham.

My phone is buzzing. On WhatsApp, my daughter Lola has said in a running commentary, 'OH MY GOD IN 89.30 WEST HAM HAVE SCORED … 3 minutes left and West Ham are winning … WOW I CAN'T BELIEVE IT!!!! Close to tears haha.' Nicola WhatsApps to say she has never seen so many grown men in tears. They have been on the phone together listening to the match, though Lola is rather worried that at this rate a lot of old men might be having heart attacks.

There's a picture of Michael, Nigel, Carolyn and Fraser celebrating in The Eagle. Even Fraser looks quite pleased for Moyes – maybe soon he'll be campaigning for a statue of him on Ilford Broadway. My old school friend Nick, a fanatical Man United fan, has texted, 'Magnificent!' People I haven't spoken to in years are getting in touch, like Robbie from Australia who says, 'Go the boys!' Scouser Gary says on Facebook, 'Every Evertonian is raising a glass tonight.' Lindsey comments simply, 'It's a miracle!' David Hills of *The Observer*, a Crystal Palace fan, emails, 'Congratulations Pete! Played havoc with our deadlines but am very pleased for you.' Steve the Cornish postie is dancing on the streets of Crantock. 'Who would have thought that claret and blue could be good for you?' declares my pal John from Bristol. Always in doubt. Absolutely always in doubt.

Obviously, West Ham getting silverware can't rank with the Moon landings or the discovery of DNA – in terms of a triumph of the human spirit it's more important than that. Amid the mayhem, it's the little moments that linger. Coufal and Souček are enjoying it in their home country and Coufal is wearing a Czech flag and celebrating with his kids. Moyes is putting his winners' medal round his dad David Sr's neck. Antonio is sitting alone in the victory arch just trying to take it all in. Micky started out at Tooting and Mitcham and is now, at the age of thirty-three, a European champion.

On the pitch, Bowen is telling the cameras:

> I spoke to my family before and said, 'Imagine scoring a goal in the last minute.' To bring a trophy to this club is the best moment of my career. The fans as well, seeing them after the game I was a bit lost for words. It's the best feeling of my life; never in my wildest dreams did I think I'd win a European trophy. I'm so buzzing, all of us are just going to go mad, I think. You have to celebrate. When the final whistle went, I just thought this party is going to be crazy. I'm just a little

> boy from Leominster who never thought I'd be talking like this. My family are crying and it just shows me how far I've come…

He is so overcome with emotion that he even resurrects a footballing cliché from the era of David Cross and Trevor Brooking:

> This is the biggest game of my career. The emotion, there was time for one more chance … I think in my position you make that run ten times, you might get that ball once. As soon as you get it you've got to put it away. I'm just so happy. I'm over the moon.

He looks at the bouncing fanbase with awe and announces, 'I'm thinking of the party tonight. Listen to it. Listen!'

Rice, always a class act, tells the pitch-side cameras:

> Honestly, it means absolutely everything. The lads have been so on it. We had a real belief. I'm not just happy for us, for the manager, but for the fans … When he [Bowen] ran through, I said out loud 'this is your time'. As soon as you see it hit the back of the net, you don't know what to do – I'm still in shock! … I absolutely love this club. They've made me one of their own. I'm just so, so happy.

He is almost tearful at times, particularly when he's asked by Joe Cole about ranking with Moore and Bonds.

> Do you know what? To be even in that conversation is crazy. I've given my heart playing for this club over the last six years. I'd give anything to help this club win. We've not had it easy. We've been facing relegation. To win this now, to be in that category potentially. I don't want to say too much. I'll get too excited.

He gives a special mention to David Moyes: 'There's been times this year when he's been tested ... But if you actually look at his time at this club ... I think he's there as West Ham's best-ever manager.'

Moyes himself is giving a slightly more sober analysis:

> I've had a long career in football and you don't get many moments like this ... It's a great moment to have my family here at the game ... The families always support you ... [West Ham is] a brilliant club in the East End of London who do brilliant work for the community. I think it's a big family club, and I think it's getting better, stronger ... Tonight's another step on the road to progress and continued progress ... This year we've gone unbeaten in Europe, which is incredible, and last year we only lost in the semi-final. Two brilliant years in

Europe – and we get another one now! We've got unbelievable support.

Bizarrely, I'm thinking of the rather sad list of trophy years that adorn the mid-tier of the London Stadium. Arsenal seemed to have hundreds of years plastered all over the Emirates but all we had was the War Cup of 1940, the FA Cup of 1964, the Cup Winners' Cup of 1965, and the FA Cups of 1975 and 1980. We could at least have added the two Second Division championship years of 1958 and 1981 and perhaps the play-off wins of 2005 and 2012 to make it look a bit better. But now we can add 2023. A trophy year, we have a trophy year!

It's an emotional moment for Denis in the stand too. He spots a tall man and asks, 'Oi, big boy, what's your name?' It turns out his name is Luděk Mikloško. He obligingly poses for selfies before presumably nipping over to nearby Moscow for a late-night lager. The normally abstemious Denis is so excited by his encounter with Ludo and West Ham winning a trophy that he allows himself to be snapped drinking a glass of celebratory chardonnay.

We head across the seats to the edge of our section and talk to Denis's pal Danny and his daughter Issy, still delirious. After forty minutes of celebrations, we watch the last players leave the field. Paquetá clutches his medal and raises a fist as he heads down the tunnel. Eventually, we head out to the UEFA buses. On the minibus back we meet another former Hammer, Bobby Barnes. He and Tony Cottee have been out in the square earlier in the day mingling with the Hammers fans. Barnes lives in Essex and is now with UEFA's ethics committee. He tells me how much the West Ham family still means to him.

Hours after the final whistle, Denis and I find ourselves in the bar of a swanky establishment called the Andaz hotel, which is where all the UEFA top brass are staying. We can see Robbie Keane and several other ex-players enjoying a post-match drink. Once safely inside, we're joined by Matt and Lisa from the fan zone and Fanis the ecstatic number one Hammers fan from Athens. He has been shouting into his phone for most of the bus journey back. Fanis has supported the Irons ever since his dad once worked on the docks in London. When I tell him that I saw West Ham win the FA Cup in 1975 and 1980 he says it is like touching history, which makes me feel a little like the Acropolis of Stratford.

Denis, fearless as ever, goes up to chat to another Hammers legend in the bar, David James, who is there as a UEFA technical observer and for some reason is carrying an Action Man figure. James looks as fit as in his playing days and proves to be a really nice, articulate fellow. He poses for a picture and tells us that the football romantic in him hopes Rice stays, as the highlight of his own career was doing something that had never been done before – winning the FA Cup with Portsmouth.

The only Premier League teams that have won trophies this season are Manchester City, Manchester United and, unbelievably, West Ham. Most fans never see their team win a major trophy. The top four and Champions League football is pretty much a closed shop, with Abu Dhabi owning Man City and Saudi Arabia's Public Investment Fund controlling Newcastle. Chelsea, Liverpool, Arsenal and Spurs have rich benefactors too. Despite the Glazers milking Man United for cash, they still spend massively on signings. Very occasionally, an outlier like Leicester City might win the league but it's looking nearly impossible for a mid-level club to break through again.

Yet, there are numerous mid-level clubs from big cities like West Ham, Aston Villa, Everton, Wolves, Leeds, the Sheffield clubs, Nottingham Forest, Middlesbrough and Sunderland hoping for a night of glory – not to mention ambitious, well-run, smaller clubs like Brighton and Brentford. Two years earlier, a group of bigger clubs tried to form a European Super League and deny the essence of football, abandoning promotion and relegation and denying the so-called smaller clubs hope. There would be no nights like this if that absurd proposal had not been defeated.

Over a cold beer or two, we all discuss what this victory means to the Hammers and decide that it's massive in terms of attracting players to a club that has won a trophy and is now in the Europa League. There is an aura of success, which feels better with each beer. At around 3 a.m. we decide it's time for bed, as Denis and I have to catch a train to Munich at 9.40 a.m. As I walk down the street to my room, disembodied cries of 'Irons!' echo from the hotel windows above. What a night. It's still hard to take in but we know what we are. Champions of Europe, I believe.

The players haven't stopped celebrating though. At around 4 a.m. my *Stop! Hammer Time* podcaster pal Mark reports that his mates Matt and Dave are in the Old Town Square, where they find the entire West Ham squad and Moyes. They grab a selfie with Bowen who is wearing an 'Irons away day' beanie hat. The squad are being led by Czech lads Souček and Coufal towards their final unspecified drinking haven.

The next day, Denis and I catch the 9.40 a.m. train from Prague – after less than five hours' sleep, but who cares? Denis is fit enough to spot Luís Figo waiting for a car and ask him for a photo – though obviously he was never good enough to play for West Ham. While buying a wrap in the organic shop at the station, I'm recognised by my Facebook friend Sam Delaney. Sam has just written a new book *Sort Your Head Out: Mental Health Without all the Bollocks*. Thanks to the events of the previous evening and the pioneering work of Dr Bowen, it seems his mental health has just taken a considerable turn for the better.

The train is packed with rather weary Hammers fans, many of them having to sit in the corridor. Our old-fashioned compartment contains Alan, a Hammers fan from Purley who travelled to Prague just to be in the fan zone and, like me, also remembers the 1976 Cup Winners' Cup final. There's a claim going round that young Divin Mubama has won more trophies than Harry Kane. While someone else has shared a meme, 'Days since a major trophy: West Ham 1, Spurs 5,583.'

Denis's mate Danny sends a WhatsApp message: 'First people I met in Berlin were two frazzled Hammers slumped in lobby of my hotel. Think we have actually taken over the world...' Alison from Clacton reports that she has 'been crying and laughing all day like a mad lady'.

West Ham winning something seems to have caused a seismic reaction throughout the UK. We're on the front pages. *The Guardian* is referring to 'Golden Hammers' and 'West Ham in dreamland'. The *Evening Standard* has 'Bowen: "This is the best feeling ever"' and 'How West Ham came to rule Europe'. Danny Dyer Sr is on YouTube saying that he actually finds the song about Jarrod Bowen and his daughter Dani quite complimentary: 'There's quite a bit of romance in it ... they're saying it can't get any better.'

Moyes has been filmed in the dressing room dancing to

'I'm Gonna Be (500 Miles)' by The Proclaimers. At this rate, he'll soon be on *Strictly Come Dancing*. Zouma appears to be twerking. Paquetá and Emerson are performing Brazilian gyrations. Coufal reveals that the players stayed up till eight in the morning before flying home. In fact, climate change, world poverty and Ukraine apart, all is for the best in the best of all possible worlds.

Six hours later at Munich airport the business class lounge is full of hungover geezers in replica West Ham shirts lying down on the sofas in what is probably not regulation business wear. On the TV monitor, BBC News has footage of Rice lifting the trophy.

Our plane must be 90 per cent full of West Ham fans. We've fared better than the fans flying from Vienna, whose plane has to turn back after encountering bad weather. We arrive at Heathrow and collapse onto the Piccadilly line, still in a state of disbelief.

While we're flying home, the players are holding their victory parade through Newham and some 70,000 fans have turned out. In a nice nod to tradition, the parade starts by the statue of World Cup winners Bobby Moore, Geoff Hurst and Martin Peters, close to West Ham's old Boleyn Ground. It goes up the Barking Road, turns right down Greengate Street towards Plaistow and finishes at Stratford Town Hall, close to the club's new home of the London Stadium.

What is being referred to as 'absolute scenes' are being

relayed on social media. Bowen is wearing a beanie hat and shades and looks a little fatigued. The players are in their claret and blue home kit and stand atop a claret double-decker bus, which has the word 'winners' emblazoned on its side. Antonio has a Jamaican flag draped round his shoulders. Green bottles of lager are being consumed. As the bus moves past the Boleyn pub, the crossroads is almost hidden beneath a mass of fans.

There's a big chant of 'Oh Saïd Benrahma!' and then everyone sings along to 'Sweet Caroline'. Plus, of course, 'West Ham are massive!' and 'Freed From Desire'. The players hold up the trophy and enjoy singing 'There's nobody better than Lucas Paquetá!' Then it's 'Just sold my car to Lucas Paquetá!' to the tune of the We Buy Any Car ads. Paquetá makes a steering wheel motion with his hands. We didn't have him down as a used car dealer in Harold Hill.

Declan performs 'Rice, rice baby!' to Vanilla Ice over the team microphone. Moyes in his shades looks like a dad trying to control a particularly rowdy stag party. Champagne is being sprayed. The trophy is nearly lost as the bus passes beneath overhanging branches. The players are waving claret and blue flares and singing 'Champione! Champione! Olé! Olé! Olé!'

Fraser and Sinead are there, standing next to an ice cream van, which does a brisk trade near the Queen's Head in West Ham Lane where the players are to get off the bus to make their final part of the journey on foot. Fraser compares it to the spirit of the 2012 London Olympics returning for one night. People are greeting neighbours and old friends they haven't seen since their schooldays. Schoolkids are climbing up fences and buildings to find a better vantage point. The police who try to stop them are booed and give up.

The buses have taken one hour and fifty minutes to get to Fraser's spot. Finally, the first of the two buses comes into view, with Rice sporting a baseball cap worn backwards and holding the cup aloft.

An exuberant Kehrer is conducting a round of community singing with the gathered masses to 'Baggy Trousers' by Madness. This might be a tribute to the ill-fitting shorts Moyes has selected to wear for the occasion, thinks Fraser. Cresswell is still looking cool, in shades and carefully groomed hair. Bowen is still in his West Ham beanie hat.

When the bus reaches Stratford Town Hall, the players take to the balcony to dance to 'Cotton Eye Joe' by Rednex. Fornals dances his way up the steps as the celebrations start all over again. Moyes is dancing to 'Is This the Way to Amarillo?'

Stratford Broadway has been closed to traffic and it's rammed with claret and blue-clad fans. Bowen still looks shocked and says, 'We just wanted to win it for the fans and look at it, it means the world.' He lifts the trophy to huge cheers. 'Freed from Desire' on the PA sees another mass celebration of his private life with Dani Dyer. Then it's 'Oh, Saïd Benrahma!' to the tune of 'Seven Nation Army'. Kehrer is hollering 'Irons!' into the microphone. Souček sings a gruff a cappella version of 'West Ham are massive!' to a sea of ecstatic faces. And now the crowd is singing 'I'm Forever Blowing Bubbles'. Just this once, West Ham really are massive. Everywhere we go.

POSTSCRIPT

Despite the glory of Prague, the inevitable happened and Declan Rice was sold to a trophy-less team in north London. There was a brief window of hope after the Europa Conference League win when he said he had two years left on his contract and 'let's just see what happens'. But in our hearts, we knew he'd go and it was hard to begrudge him Champions League football and the chance of a title push. Though it would have been easier if he'd departed to Manchester City or Bayern Munich, rather than a direct London rival in Arsenal. Particularly as my house is so close to the Emirates Stadium.

The deal seemed to take for ever once the clubs fixed a fee of £105 million. It took around two weeks for the lawyers to finalise various contract details before the distressing pictures finally emerged of Rice in an Arsenal shirt. West Ham had done well to negotiate the fee up from an initial £80 million offer, but the big question was: how would the club spend the money?

A period of stasis followed with no activity, and the club seemingly in danger of losing the transfer window. Tim Steidten had been recruited as technical director from Bayer Leverkusen. There were rumours, probably exaggerated in the media, of Moyes and Steidten disagreeing on potential transfer targets. A doomed pursuit of Manchester United's Harry Maguire ended with the man nicknamed 'Slabhead' rejecting the Irons. With no new signings, a lot of fans, who presumably did not go to Prague, completely lost their sense of proportion on social media. After a friendly defeat to Bayer Leverkusen, there were bizarre calls from some for Moyes and/or Steidten to be sacked.

But finally, in August there was transfer activity. At last, the club agreed a £32 million fee with Ajax for defensive midfielder Edson Álvarez, a Mexican international. Then along came James Ward-Prowse, who had been rumoured to be signing all summer, arriving from Southampton for a bargain £30 million. We all knew about his free kicks already, but he was a great team player and good professional too.

Next came a massive signing – in terms of letters, at least. Promising young centre-back Konstantinos Mavropanos came from Stuttgart for £20 million, the first Greek international to play for West Ham. The last deal before the transfer window closed saw the club finally get some Kudus, with the

Hammers agreeing a £38 million deal with Ajax for Mohammed Kudus. The Ghanaian international was a hugely promising attacking midfielder who could also do a job up front.

There was also a significant departure, with last summer's great hope Gianluca Scamacca heading back to Italy with Atalanta for a fee of £27 million. Michail Antonio had previously seen off the £45 million Sébastien Haller and there seems to be an unwritten rule that he will always be the main striker at West Ham.

But for all the promising signings, it suddenly emerged that Manchester City were interested in buying Lucas Paquetá. To lose both Rice and Paquetá after the Europa Conference League win would have been a significant blow. But thankfully for the Hammers, City withdrew their interest when it emerged that Paquetá was being investigated by the FA over suspicious betting activity concerning his yellow cards – allegations he denied. Paquetá seemed inspired after that, and whatever his disappointment over the failed move, turned in some brilliant performances for West Ham.

The Irons started the season with the new-found confidence of having won a trophy. Bowen, who had not scored in any away games the previous season, scored in each of his first seven away games. Álvarez, Rice's replacement, was a strong and combative midfielder who stuck to his defensive job; this seemed to liberate Tomáš Souček, who started to score again.

Never mind the free kicks of Ward-Prowse, his corners seemed as good as a goal, swinging unerringly on to a Hammers head. The man whose name sounds like a firm of solicitors on Brentwood High Street was getting goals from open play and several assists – an early candidate for signing of the season. Kudus was unleashed from the bench and scored a great leveller against Newcastle and a brilliant bicycle kick at Brentford. Rice was irreplaceable but the four signings made with the money had hopefully strengthened the squad overall.

After four games, West Ham were top of the Premier League – for a Friday night at least – after winning at Luton. We knew it was likely to be a better season in the Premier League when West Ham went to Brighton and won with three classic counter-attacking goals – an event about as likely as lightning striking the ArcelorMittal Orbit twice on successive Saturdays. The Europa League campaign began with West Ham winning their group after five matches. Paquetá scored with a towering header at Freiberg in Germany where West Ham played without any away supporters, the club's fans having been banned for one game after the missile throwing in Prague.

Loyalty isn't something you associate with modern footballers. So, another major boost has been Bowen being on hire and signing a new seven-year contract – and probably becoming Essex royalty in the process. He said:

> This club gave me the opportunity when no one else wanted to. Without this club, I wouldn't have played for my country and I wouldn't have scored the winning goal in a European final. So I think it's only fair that I repay that faith. I want to stay here and I want to stay here for the rest of my career.

Of course, this being West Ham, a poor run then followed before results improved again. We beat Declan Rice's Arsenal in the Carabao Cup and won at Spurs. It could yet all go wrong, and we might be in a relegation struggle by the time you read this, with the London Stadium inundated by a tsunami on the River Lee, David Moyes injured on *Strictly*, twenty-five players on the injury list and Mark Noble having to make an unlikely comeback. But as I write this, the signs are that the club might be making some progress. There's a sense of togetherness among the players who celebrated long into the Prague night. Could it be that we won't have to wait another forty-three years for a trophy?

Come on you Irons!

Pete May
December 2023

ACKNOWLEDGEMENTS

Firstly, thanks to all those who have endured forty-three years of hurt with me over the years at West Ham, including current companions Matt George, Lisa Pritchard, Fraser Massey, Nigel Morris and Michael McManus. Gavin Hadland, Big Sam, Carolyn Quinn, Alison O'Brien, Scott O'Brien and Steve Flory all played their part as members of the matchday squad in the 2022–23 season.

A massive thank you must go to Denis Campbell for somehow getting me to the Europa Conference League final against all odds. He is now guaranteed a lifetime of jellied eels, right royal knees-ups and other assorted cockney clichés round at my gaff. Denis's wife Clare Finnigan was also a brilliant travel facilitator.

Thanks to David Hills and Jon Brodkin for publishing my West Ham views in *The Guardian* and *The Observer* and to all those who have read and commented on my blog *Hammers in the Heart*, hammersintheheart.blogspot.com. Thanks also to Phil Whelans and Mark Gower from the *Stop! Hammer Time* podcast for allowing me the oxygen of publicity and giving background information on their own trips to Prague. Matt and Lisa provided colour from the fan zone and Fraser from the parade. Joe Norris deserves great credit for facilitating a trip to the seaside for our annual drubbing at Brighton, as does Michael the Gooner for enabling me to infiltrate the Arsenal North Bank. Sinead and all the staff at The Eagle must be praised for providing post-match refreshments.

I'm indebted to my wife Nicola Baird and daughters Lola May and Nell May for persevering with my years of dreaming that West Ham might win a trophy and for providing support and solace on matchdays.

Finally, a big thank you to Phill Jupitus and Iain Dale for the cover quotes, James Stephens at Biteback for commissioning this book and Catriona Allon for her painstaking editing. You've all been massive!

ABOUT THE AUTHOR

Pete May's previous books on West Ham include *Goodbye to Boleyn*, *Hammers in the Heart* and *West Ham: Irons in the Soul*. His other books include *The Joy of Essex*, *Summit for the Week-end*, *Man About Tarn*, *What Are Words Worth?*, *Whovian Dad*, *There's a Hippo in my Cistern* and *Sunday Muddy Sunday*. As a journalist, he has written for *The Guardian*, *The Observer*, *The Independent*, *New Statesman*, *Loaded*, *Time Out*, *Mid-week* and many other publications. He is married with two daughters, a border terrier and a large collection of West Ham programmes in the attic. Once an Essex man, he now lives in north London.